Radical Analysis

Special Education

371.92

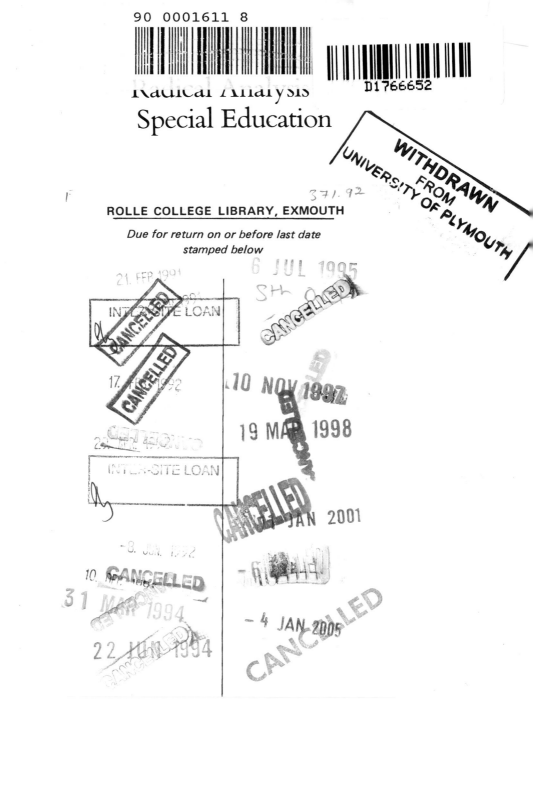

Radical Analysis of Special Education:

Focus on Historical Development and Learning Disabilities

Scott B. Sigmon

 The Falmer Press

(A member of the Taylor & Francis Group)
London, New York and Philadelphia

UK   The Falmer Press, Falmer House, Barcombe, Lewes, East Sussex, BN8 5DL

USA   The Falmer Press, Taylor & Francis Inc., 242 Cherry Street, Philadelphia, PA 19106-1906

First published in 1987

British Library Cataloging in Publication Data

Sigmon, Scott B.
   Radical analysis of special education: focus on historical
   development and learning disabilities.
    1. Exceptional children—Education—United States—History.
    2. Learning disabilities—United States.
    3. Educational sociology.
    I. Title
   371.9'0973   LC4705
   ISBN 1-85002-30-4
   ISBN 1-85002-31-2 (Pbk.)

Typeset in 11/13 Bembo by
Alresford Typesetting & Design, New Farm Road, Alresford, Hants.

Printed in Great Britain by Taylor & Francis (Printers) Ltd, Basingstoke, Hants.

Contents

List of Tables

Acknowledgement

Chapter 2 in this work is a revision of S.B. Sigmon's 'The history and future of educational segregation' (*Journal for Special Educators*, Summer 1983). Used with permission of PRO-ED, Austin, TX.

Dedications

To Victor (Jean Itard's 'wild boy of Aveyron'), not usually stated, but perhaps the first modern and most famous special education student; to Jim Giarelli and Gerry Coles for scholarly inspiration; to Joan Loughman for fine typing; to my mother Shirley Juffe Sigmon for spiritual and material support; and to Robin.

Foreword

In the face of harm to children, silence is complicity and self-betrayal.
                                                        Author unknown

This work has been done by a practicing school psychologist concerned with problems in special education today and what caused them. The problems became obvious through first hand professional experience, and their causes were uncovered mainly through historical research. The research formally began during the author's graduate studies and culminated with his doctoral dissertation at Rutgers University upon which this book is primarily based.

This book is, hopefully, in some measure, a systematic reading of the non-educational purposes of current special education interventions. It is also a practical case study, to some degree, on the 'specific learning disability' label since it is the newest yet largest special education category in terms of the number of children actually classified. This is also a study, to some lesser extent, on the follies of current practices for dealing with the so-called 'mildly educationally handicapped' student.

American special education has become so pervasive that the field requires critical analysis. Not only do the ethics of certain existing practices demand major attention, but even more pressing is the basic question: When is a child special or exceptional enough to warrant differential education? The latter is most important to this work. Moral education has been very popular among philosophers of education recently; perhaps special education may also become so, some time in the not too distant future.

The major objectives of this study were to present facts in an original way, but also to induce major changes in American educational policy. Moreover, this work is a vehicle of thought. History is the road, philosophy of education forms the wheels, sociology of education the body, and school psychology the engine. An excursion will be taken from the earliest historical roots of American special education to some of the most serious issues in the field today. A radical perspective on all of this will be constructed. This excursion will probably cause a motion sickness in thought for those who believe that American society is fine just the way it is or for those who feel the same way about American education, general or special. Research and personal experience have taught me otherwise, especially in regard to contemporary American special education.

Scott B. Sigmon, Ed.D.
Union, New Jersey, USA
December, 1986

Chapter 1

Introduction

There is a continuing need for a Marxist analysis of many topics not discussed or just touched upon in this book, such as . . . learning disabilities.

Joseph Nahem (1981, *Psychology and psychiatry today: A Marxist view*, p. 4)

Background

This work will be a radical analysis of American special education generally, with a specific focus on the concept of 'learning disabilities' (LD). There has not been a lengthy treatment of American special education utilizing a radical perspective. Also, since the notion of learning disabilities is a burning current issue in American education, it provides a logical center for a comprehensive analysis of special education.

For the purposes of this study, radical is defined as an appeal to 'roots' or 'basic elements'. A radical educational analysis focuses on the roots or basic elements underlying educational processes. What are the 'roots' of educational processes? Education is always a process of conserving, creating and criticizing culture. Culture is not only 'lived experiences functioning within the context of historically located structures and social formations', as it has been traditionally defined; but also '"lived antagonistic relations" situated within a complex of socio-political institutions and social forms that limit as well as enable human action' (Giroux, 1981, p. 26). Giroux's addendum to the traditional view of culture adds immeasurably to its political significance. Giroux shows that culture can be seen no longer as something neutral functioning 'out there' to be studied in a naive *in vacuo* way or in the fashion of an apologist for the status quo. Therefore, a radical critique of education is an analysis of the social, economic, and political foundations of cultural transmission practices. In essence then, this research will cover, in part, how the political form affects educational arrangements in general and special education in particular. Giroux (1981) exemplifies well the relationship of radical political thinking and schooling: 'The truth of radical pedagogy lies in its power to negate the power of those who define what is legitimate and real' (p. 79).

Focusing primarily on the concept of learning disabilities within a radical critique of American special education is particularly germane for three reasons: (a) Much of contemporary special educational practice, research, and professional literature has been devoted to learning disabilities; (b) the belief in the very existence of a learning disability syndrome has been questioned over the past several years within professional journals from such fields as education, special education, and orthopsychiatry; and (c) if the learning disability syndrome is myth, even partially, special education has been greatly misdirected. Thus, this is a crucial area of study because of its practical and theoretical implications for change in special education and American education as a whole.

Previous studies of American special education have been basically attempts at 'neutral' historical or empirical quantitative description and limited in the kinds of conclusions that could be culled. Special education needs a systematic overview combined with a radical analysis of cultural transmissions to achieve new understanding. Because special education has been studied previously through restricted modes of inquiry, its underlying social, economic, and political roots have not been exposed. Therefore, after cutting through the foliage, what remains to be examined are the social functions of the contemporary concept of learning disabilities and the ultimate role of special education in a free society.

From the outset it should be made clear that this writer is a staunch supporter of special education. Yet at the same time the position taken here is that special education has been perverted. It is believed that special education should serve only truly educationally handicapped students. The primary purpose of this work is to examine who receives special education and why, while the major thesis is that much of what passes for American special education today is misguided and dysfunctional. This will be elucidated by exploring the historical development of special education and issues of current import from a radical social and educational perspective. The phrase 'special needs' — probably used more frequently in the United Kingdom (UK) than in the United States when characterizing educationally handicapped students — is utilized here to emphasize how rhetoric supports ideology. Tomlinson (1982) writes:

> The terminology used as a legitimation for the exclusion of more and more children from the normal education system and for placing them in a type of education which does not allow them to compete for educational credentials, and subjects them to even more

social control than in normal schooling, is that of special needs. The use of the term is rapidly becoming tautological rhetoric, and its uses are more ideological than educational. (Tomlinson, 1982, p. 72).

Tomlinson claims that 'educational need' is an ambiguous term, and was originally inspired by J.J. Rousseau's (*Emile*, 1974) distinction between true and artificial needs when discussing his mythical pupil Emile: 'give him not what he wants but what he needs'. The reference to Rousseau may be stretching thin a point, but the growing numbers of students formally labeled for special educational programming is a well documented fact in the USA which will be discussed later.

While this writer agrees with Tomlinson's notion that the term special needs is being applied more and more to students for purposes of subjecting them to special educational 'treatment', it can be argued that certain students are easily recognized as having special needs that must be addressed to help them to receive any education whatsoever. There is no mention of Emile being handicapped in any of Rousseau's writings. He was, in fact, quite privileged in that he received the sole attention of a very learned teacher. It could be said, though, that he was disadvantaged because his education was censored and isolated. On the other hand, children who are deaf, blind, or orthopedically disabled are much more likely to have legitimate special needs, although they all may not necessarily require a special education. The problem of determining what is a special need becomes problematic when dealing with children who have no external physical abnormality and this is the heart of the special education controversy today.

Many children today are being classified as educationally handicapped and receiving some form of special education even though they give the outward bodily impression of being perfectly normal. These children are classified on the basis of inferential information. There has been an enormous number of children across the USA classified as being educationally handicapped in recent years, mostly based on inferential test data. The numbers are so large that children classified based upon inferential data have been referred to commonly as 'high incidence' handicapped youngsters. The higher incidence handicapping conditions are learning disabilities (LD), emotional disturbance (ED), and mild or educable mental retardation (EMR). On the other hand, deafness, blindness, and physical deformity, which are obvious conditions, are, fortunately, not too common and are known as 'low incidence' handicaps.

Although strong rumblings regarding the learning disability (LD) label have been felt from time to time since the mid to late 1970s (Algozzine and Sutherland, 1977; Coles, 1978; Divoky, 1974; Schrag and Divoky, 1975), the LD controversy is beginning to erupt in the mid-1980s and may very well shake the foundations of American education. Because of the growing concern over the increase in use of the LD label, a number of diverse educational groups and educational publications are starting to seriously address this issue. For instance, a symposium on the nature of the LD label (Algozzine and Abrams, 1984) was listed as one of three 'convention highlights' at the 1984 annual meeting of the National Association of School Psychologists (NASP). This is especially important since the membership of this group is directly involved in making LD diagnoses. Conservative educational critics (e.g., Gardner, 1984) have recently complained about the large sums of money spent on special education and especially for LD students. *Education Week*, which frequently reaches a wide audience within the American national education community, in one issue featured two front page articles on the LD controversy (Foster, 1984; Loeb, 1984). Although not solely directed at the LD label, regarding special education, the mayor of the city of New York 'said he was concerned about the increasing size and cost of the city's special-education program. . . . saying the program had "failed in its mission", largely because it had been unsuccessful in moving children into regular classes' ('Koch Appoints', 1984, p. 47). The latter reference here is to the supposed temporary nature of special placement of children with minor impairments — which has been a potent rationale of long standing — many of whom never find their way back completely or at all to regular educational programming. Lastly in this vein, influential child advocacy groups — which formerly were concerned primarily with over-representation of minority students in classes for the mildly retarded and concomitant biased assessment — are starting to become very interested in the LD issue (Radford-Hill, 1984).

A humanitarian endeavor, to this author's way of thinking, is when scarce resources (time, money, effort, or materiel) are expended to help other, needy humans. It is much more difficult to build a case for humanitarianism when something is done for an individual or group after it is mandated by litigation which later results in legislation, or when the resources provided are a meager philanthropic gesture. Contrary to popular opinion, special education did not come about so much for humanitarian reasons, but rather evolved due to the inability of a mass, compulsory general education system to deal effectively with moderately to severely handicapped students. Originally, special education was private, voluntary, and minuscule in scope in terms of numbers served, and not necessarily geared for children. This writer is of the opinion that not enough is properly done for or spent on the more seriously handicapped students. Conclusions regarding the special educational treatment of millions of 'mildly' handicapped youngsters will be more appropriately discussed later after reviewing in depth the current situation and what led up to it.

Statement of the Problem

The large number of schoolchildren formally classified as having some form of mild educationally handicapping condition is alarming, rapidly growing, and very well may be the most serious practical as well as ethical dilemma confronting American educators. The label most often assigned to such children is 'specific learning disability' (LD), as broadly defined by the federal government. The result for these children is placement in various special educational tracks. The dramatic growth in the number of LD pupils raises many problems, including: (a) the validity of the LD syndrome itself, (b) the population being labeled, and (c) the necessity of labeling a student having only a mild learning problem before additional help can be provided. The primary problem is that special education, by way of LD schooling tracks, has been perverted into a means of child control.

To help see through the current special education morass — which has really come together through upheavals of previous attitudes and social conditions — a different way of looking at the current state of affairs is necessary. In the past, work in special education has been done in either one of two ways. On the one hand, there is the quantitative, empirical technique generally utilized in behavioral psychology to scientifically examine phenomena. On the other hand, there is the functional approach usually associated with traditional sociology that has a tendency to justify existing arrangements. Advances in thought often require a different point of view.

For this work, a different research paradigm drawn from radical perspectives in sociology, history, and philosophy has been borrowed, and modified somewhat to suit the intended purposes here. From this perspective, special education can be seen with its underlying social, economic, and political roots unearthed. As such, fresh insights can be gained. Recommendations for future policy for special education from a new perspective can then be offered.

The major objectives of this work are to systematically examine the ideological and social purposes of the learning disabilities (LD) concept within the framework of American special education as well as to trace its historical and conceptual development. Ideological purpose here means justifying the existence of some body of ideas on which a particular political, economic, or social system is based. It is important for this work to find special education's intellectual sources and to see how it has changed over time because of LD.

The main thesis is that there are dramatic confrontations in the wind — not only between the (learning disabilities specialist) field and government policy-makers, but also between scholars, researchers, and practitioners who have vastly different conceptualizations and intellectual interests (not to mention career interests) at stake in any debate about the viability of the learning disability label. An important related thesis is that the LD category of American special education, in its present form, will probably fall victim to the same type of political and social pressures that the Educable Mentally Retarded (EMR), and to some lesser extent the Emotionally Disturbed (ED), labels did; but this is not necessarily an example of over-zealous social policy run amok. Rather, the LD category is running a cyclical course, it filled a void in American education, and it has been over-used as well as abused. Another thesis is that the LD concept emerged with great popularity at a time after EMR special self-contained classes had been widely accepted (around the 1950s), and because there were still many children who were not learning but were apparently too bright to be placed in EMR classes. Further, around this time, much professional attention had gone into studying methods for teaching the 'slow learner'. The slow learner period (late 1950s and 1960s) has really been quite over-looked, yet this seems to have been the precursor and/or impetus to the LD movement. Additionally, the LD label, which is said to be of biological genesis, appears to have served a social function.

Now that the EMR controversy has died down somewhat, it seems as though the LD label has received greater attention. This focused attention has not all been favorable, and this is what has allowed the LD controversy to emerge.

Other theses are that LD grew out of previously entrenched areas of special education (e.g., mental retardation and physical disabilities) and from the 'medical model' which has been associated with the study of handicapped students. An LD classification has been used to provide children with special education who do not function well in regular educational programs, many of whom are not handicapped in any intrapsychic or physical way. Since the number of children classified LD has been growing dramatically, the LD classification becomes more ideologically laden. It is likely that a substantial number of low socioeconomic status children are provided special education when in fact they might actually need remediation, bilingual education, or just an academic foundation (of scope and sequence). Perhaps students are classified LD because it is too easy to get money for this category of youngster from the federal government.

Questions of the Study

The major questions which drive this study are as follows. What are the historical roots of American special education? What are the historical and social roots of the concept of learning disabilities (LD)? What are the social and historical roots of the LD controversy and how would a radical socioeducational analysis (RSA) explain it? What are the implications of an RSA for American special education, the LD controversy, and future practice and policy?

Method: Radical Socioeducational Analysis (RSA)

Liberal and conservative ideologies — which have been dominant in capitalist societies — find expression in the 'functional paradigm' which stresses:

> the positive . . . essential functions of schooling in an increasingly complex and meritocratic society. Schools teach cognitive skills and cosmopolitan values in attitudes; they represent an essentially rational way of sorting and selecting talent in a society that more and more demands competence and expertise for the effective performance of occupational roles. (Hurn, 1978, p. 53)

Both liberals and conservatives have failed to connect the history and practice of schooling consistently with larger structures of power and social class. On the other hand, the 'radical paradigm sees schools as serving the interests of elites, as reinforcing existing inequalities, and as producing attitudes that foster acceptance of this status quo' (Hurn, 1978, p. 44). With the radical perspective developed in the last decade or so we have been presented with another perspective on the history and practice of education which attempts to explain through radical analysis the roots of cultural transmission. These radical perspectives have provided a unique view of the problem of education as well as the possibilities for change.

With very few exceptions, special education has not enjoyed the unique insights to be gained from this radical analysis. It is only sensible to think that special education, like all other education, is rooted also in larger structures of power, ideology, etc. If special education is to understand its history and present fundamentally so as to develop a sound basis for future policy, it too needs a radical analysis. A radical perspective will be utilized to interpret the historical development of American special education and the place of learning disabilities (LD) within it.

Giarelli (1982) points out that there is disagreement in the methods and conclusions of radical educational critics despite strong commonalities in their work. However, Giarelli (1982) uses the phrase 'fundamental radical analysis' when discussing 'the linkages between economic and cultural institutions' which 'form the basis for any radical educational theory'

(p. 465). This author utilizes another variation of fundamental radical analysis, herein called radical socioeducational analysis (RSA). RSA emphasizes historical development within the social context, the difficulty (or perhaps the impossibility) of value-free social science, and Karl Marx's (1818–1883) notion of the dialectic within the realm of social class conflict theory.

In essence then, this work is both an interpretive and historical study. The method is *qualitative*, as opposed to quantitative. RSA is an interactive-interdisciplinary way of looking at the social conditions which impinge upon schooling or education and which in turn impact upon the social facts of life. It is interdisciplinary in that RSA is a flexible open system and interactive or reciprocal as in Marx's dialectical framework. RSA is not based upon truly unique thought on the part of the author, although the term RSA probably is original (see Sigmon, 1985 a, for an extensive explication of the underlying 'weltanschauung' of RSA). Rather, RSA is a synthesis arrived at from previous radical thinkers.

Marx used history as a sociological tool. History is the road on which a radical socioeducational analysis moves. 'For we must turn to history in order to understand the traditions that have shaped our individual biographies and intersubjective relationships with other human beings' (Giroux, 1981, p. 57). Existing are 'suppression of historical consciousness in the social sphere and the loss of interest in history in the sphere of schooling in the United States at the present time' (Giroux, 1981, p. 40). More emphasis on history can lead to better understanding of our present circumstances and a greater likelihood of more humane social relationships.

Marx, a realist materialist, adapted from the idealist philosopher Hegel the method of dialectical logic and applied it to observable social and economic processes — to what is commonly known as 'political economy' and to what this writer calls 'historical socioeconomic studies'. Unlike traditional a-historical logic of Eleatic philosophers which is concerned with nontemporal conditions, dialectical logic alone is a mode of thinking that can deal with change, development, and history (Riegel, 1979). Although dialectical logic was not the simplistic notion of thesis-antithesis-synthesis for either Hegel (Buss, 1979), or Marx, the latter did look at socioeconomic tensions, harmonies, and their outcomes.

RSA, like conventional methods of inquiry, is for studying what is; but also, RSA is the study of why and what could be and how. This is to deny any claim of being value-free. Humans are a product of their total experiences which in turn shape their values. An honest, intelligent appraisal is the goal of an RSA. Thus, as radical here means an appeal to 'roots' or 'basic elements', a radical socioeducational analysis focuses on the roots or basic elements underlying educational processes. In this research an effort is made to avoid the trap of contemporary quantitative-statistical empiricism (and the functional paradigm) whereby the method is thought to be value-free and completely objective. Multi-dimensional social factors impinge upon the individual which cannot be 'held constant' or 'factored out'.

Review of Selected Literature

Social Philosophies and Education

'*Modern liberalism*' is a social philosophy that is future oriented and engenders slow reform. The liberal thinks that education will benevolently transform society. It stresses public (governmental) spending on social programs (Gill, 1980).

'Classic liberalism' is today actually '*conservatism*'. The conservative believes that there is within the universe a 'fixed grand plan', and as such, is resistant to change. Conservatism is usually associated with the economic arrangement of capitalism. Education, then, in this scheme of things, is a social arrangement in which the plan can be perpetuated. (See Brann's, 1979, implicitly conservative position on education; and also Damico's, 1978, discussion of the neoconservative).

Radical critiques on education, or more specifically schooling, are not new. Socrates criticized the Sophists in the fourth century BC (Lucas, 1972), and there were probably many unknown school critics before him — probably beginning right after the notion of education was first conceptualized. Major innovations concerning teaching methods and vast changes in schooling arrangements are called radical. Politically, seeking a much different form of government is referred to as being radical. This research will consider the implications of the 'new' and the 'vast', but here, radical means 'basic' or 'root elements'. It is believed, though, that fundamental social and economic change through new political arrangements will have greater impact upon schooling than is possible under the current political system.

The radical critiques of education in recent times have come from a diverse group including classroom teachers, philosophers of education, and a host of critical social theorists. Some wanted to radicalize the classroom (Postman and Weingartner, 1969), begin alternative schools (Gross and Gross, 1969), and discuss social relations in school from a humanistic slant (Neill, 1960). Others focused on curriculum or dealt with the shortcomings of society as a whole but with a more modern argument (Apple, 1979; Bowles and Gintis, 1976; Levitas, 1974; Sharp, 1980). Moreover, Ivan Illich

(1970) is so pessimistic about improving traditional schools that he wants to do away with them altogether and set up other educational arrangements. Illich's 'deschooling' notion has been branded, among other things, as radical Catholicism (Reagan, 1980), participatory socialism (Hedman, 1979), and small-scale entrepreneurial — as opposed to corporate — capitalism (Bowles and Gintis, 1976). Deschooling is said to have evolved out of the freeschooling movement (Wasserman, 1974). In essence, deschoolers want to carry on the task of education in a voluntary and more decentralized way using whatever technology is available; and they believe that school is not the great equalizer, it produces shortages of skilled persons and creates too much unwarranted public trust in certificates which schools award. Finally, no review of modern radical educational thought would be complete without mentioning Paulo Freire (1970) who discusses the political functions of education, consciousness raising, and based *in vivo* pedagogical projects on the actual experiences of his illiterate peasant adult students.

In the past it had been generally assumed that certain socio-political arrangements generated certain types of educational arrangements. This sort of relationship was assumed to be so axiomatic that specific focus or intellectual energy was not spent in examining particular aspects of school-ing — at least from a leftist point of view for the most part. Many Marxists, in particular, see any sort of noncommunist government-controlled school-ing as a nefarious ideological tool of the state that is not worth examining since the school system cannot adequately be changed until the govern-mental form is totally replaced.

More recently, some noteworthy leftist intellectual and practical activity has addressed specific educational problems at the micro-level while acknowledging that there are major shortcomings with society as a whole. The foundation for this sort of radical critique comes from two main foundations generally referred to as 'the new sociology of education' and 'Marxist criticism on education'. In 1971 the 'new' sociology of education was born with the publication of *Knowledge and control: New directions for the sociology of education* (Young, 1971) from the UK. In the introductory chapter, aptly titled 'Knowledge and control', Young writes about the book's other authors who 'do not take for granted existing definitions of educational reality, and therefore do "make" rather than "take" problems for the sociology of education. They are inevitably led to consider. . . . "what counts as educational knowledge" as problematic' (pp. 2–3). Young — in paraphrasing Alan F. Blum who wrote chapter four which is called 'The corpus of knowledge as a normative order' — explicates how, to proceed at all, 'sociologists (and by implication other knowledge practitioners) accept a "common culture" which is never described or analysed by them' (p. 9). 'Control' is viewed as the 'imposition of meaning' which Young credits to Dawe (1970). *Knowledge and control* is concerned with curricula (part one), what counts as knowledge (part two), and 'cognitive styles in comparative perspective', intra- and cross-culturally (part three). Regarding these three (and all other as of yet unnamed concerns) Young wrote 'are in no sense exhaustive of the possible problems raised for the sociological enquiry in education by treating knowledge and control as problematic' (p. 7). As can be gleaned from these few small quotes, new ground was being broken here. Further, the stage was being set to cover other concerns, i.e., special education programs. Why not analyze its 'common culture'? Too much has been accepted about special educational ideas without question. Sarup's (1978) *Marxism and education: A study of phenomenological and Marxist approaches to education* and Harris' (1979) *Education and knowledge: The structured misrepresentation of reality* are of this family of thought and were also published in England (although Harris is an Australian). Sarup refers to his book as 'new' sociology of education while Harris wrote 'If this work could carry a second sub-title, that sub-title would in all probability be: "A New Introduction to Philosophy of Education" ' (p. vii). Although Sarup claims to be coming from the field of the 'new' sociology of education and Harris that of a 'new philosophy of education', they actually reach a convergence via the material they deem important for educational studies and through their methodology.

Similar work has been done recently in the USA. Two exceptionally comprehensive book reviews found in philosophy of education-oriented journals by Giroux (1980) and Giarelli (1982) point out the inadequacies of some radical education critiques and provide detailed surveys on the new sociology of education (especially the former) and Marxist criticism of education (more so the latter). Two books by Henry A. Giroux (1981, 1983) put forth the modern conception of radical thinking and education. Giroux does a masterful job of tying together a number of threads of contemporary radical thought with schooling. Giroux's material is most important because he focuses on ideology. In the past, school problems were usually approached in terms of the superstructure (social philosophy) and the nuts and bolts (curriculum, methods, programs, etc.) but without the ideology which is the nexus that ties them both together.

Special Education

The following are classic special education texts written by persons who helped shape the field. In William M. Cruickshank and G. Orville Johnson's (1967) *Education of exceptional children and youth*, Chapter 1 by Cruickshank is quite important: 'The development of education for exceptional children'. Lloyd M. Dunn's (1973) *Exceptional children in the schools: Special education in transition* covers changes in special educational programs for handicapped youngsters. It delves into the social ramifications of the issues pertaining to the schooling of atypical youngsters. Lastly, Robinson and Robinson's (1965) book, *The mentally retarded child: A psychological approach*, is extremely well written and provides some important historical material about special education.

There is also recent research literature that brings together the socio-political with the special educational domain. For example, 'An analysis of the incidence of special class placement: The masses are burgeoning' (Algozzine, Ysseldyke and Christensen, 1983), 'A three-tiered model for the assessment of culturally and linguistically different children' (Brady, Manni and Winikur, 1983), 'Biological determinism and the ideological roots of student classification' (Selden, 1983), 'Society, ideology and the reform of special education: A study in the limits of educational change' (Shapiro, 1980), and 'The history and future of educational segregation' (Sigmon, 1983 a). The titles are rather self-explanatory, show the kinds of issues appearing recently in scholarly journals, and ultimately can help provide a better understanding of the relationship of special education to ideology.

Learning Disabilities

The origins of the notion of specific learning disabilities (LD) can be traced to the work with the retarded and the brain damaged beginning in the early 1930s (Hallahan and Cruickshank, 1973). The field became formalized largely through the efforts of Samuel A.Kirk who started using the term 'learning disabilities' in the early 1960s 'which had been put forth more or less accidentally by parents' (Cruickshank, 1983, p. 191). Kirk invited some research-educator professionals who had been interested in brain damaged and retarded students to join him for a meeting at a hotel room in Chicago in 1964 (which Cruickshank attended). It was here where the term LD gained acceptance by leaders from within special education and a new professional subspecialty was born. Kirk and Bateman's (1962) slightly earlier conceptualization was adopted by convention as the standard LD definition:

> A *learning disability* refers to a retardation, disorder, or delayed development in one or more of the processes of speech, language, reading, writing, arithmetic, or other school subjects resulting from a psychological handicap caused by a possible cerebral dysfunction and/or emotional or behavioral disturbances. It is not the result of

mental retardation, sensory deprivation, or cultural or instructional factors. (p. 73)

The US federal government later adopted a similar, broad definition of 'special learning disabilities' (National Advisory Committee, 1968) but it was more precise in delineating who was not in this category: 'Such term does not include children who have learning problems which are primarily the result of visual, hearing, or motor handicaps, or mental retardation, of emotional disturbance, or of environmental, cultural, or economic disadvantage' (p. 14).

Classic texts by leaders in the field of learning disabilities that provide a solid foundation in terms of how LD was 'conventionally viewed' prior to the recent controversy of the last few years are: *Learning disabilities* (McCarthy and McCarthy, 1969), *Psychoeducational foundations of learning disabilities* (Hallahan and Cruickshank, 1973), *Introduction to learning disabilities: A psycho-behavioral approach* (Hallahan and Kauffman, 1976), and *Learning disabilities: Selected ACLD papers* (Kirk and McCarthy, 1975), the latter being an edited book with presented convention papers about LD from 1963 to 1974 by many authors.

The professional honeymoon that began in the early 1960s with consensus among educators regarding LD is in the mid-1980s resulting in abrupt separation or even outright divorce. There has been a growing number of articles over the past few years within the professional literature questioning: the number of American students classified as having LD (Algozzine *et al.*, 1983), the efficacy of tests to diagnose LD (Coles, 1978), whether learning disabilities actually exist at all (McKnight, 1982) and American theory regarding learning disabilities which is said to be 'reductionist, unproven, and fails to provide a theoretical basis for the understanding of these problems' (Coles, 1983, p. 619). The degree to which writers explicitly mention any connection between learning disabilities and ideology appears to be, not surprisingly, a function both of vested professional interests and political leanings. There are many writers who still believe strongly that even very mild inferential learning disabilities do exist, and that learning disabled children should be placed in special classes with a low pupil-teacher ratio. Cruickshank (1983) feels that problems within the field of learning disabilities *per se* are due to poor research and professional competitiveness.

Finally, some publications, most all of which are recent articles, specifically concerning the 'learning disabilities controversy', provide a basic understanding of what is now taking place within the field and will enable documentation of something very significant in American education. These publications include what this writer views as three basic types: (a) the hostile, primarily to the formal classification itself and its implications; (b) the reconciliatory, primarily by persons most closely professionally associated with special education and especially with learning disabilities; and (c) those that appeal positively for a reformulation of theory. All three types do overlap somewhat. Examples of the three types above are, respectively: (a) 'The politics and science of learning disability classification: Implications for black children' (Collins and Camblin, 1983), 'The learning disability myth in American education' (McKnight, 1982), *The myth of the hyperactive child: And other means of child control* (Schrag and Divoky, 1975); (b) 'On the heels of psychology' (Blatt, 1982), 'Straight is the bamboo tree' (Cruickshank, 1983), 'Neuropsychological subtyping of learning-disabled children: History, methods, implications' (Fisk and Rourke, 1983); and (c) 'Learning disabilities as a subset of school failure: The oversophistication of a concept' (Algozzine and Ysseldyke, 1983); 'The use of Soviet psychological theory in understanding learning dysfunctions' (Coles, 1983), 'Similarities and differences between low achievers and students classified learning disabled' (Ysseldyke, Algozzine, Shinn and McGue, 1982). The hostile position toward learning disabilities is well characterized by Schrag and Divoky (1975) in their chapter entitled 'The invention of a disease'. They also delineate reasons for confusion and disagreement about LD in the passage following.

> In less than a decade, the ailment spread from virtual obscurity to something of epidemic proportions. It has no single name, no universally accepted symptoms, and no discernible anatomical or biochemical characteristics. . . . Its most common name, not surprisingly, is 'learning disabilities' (LD) but it is also associated, sometimes synonymously, with 'minimal brain dysfunction' (MBD), 'hyperkinesis', 'impulse disorder' and a substantial number of other conditions and 'syndromes'. Before 1965 almost no one had heard of it, but by the beginning of the seventies it was commanding the attention of an armada of pediatricians, neurologists and educational psychologists, and by mid-decade, pedagogical theory, medical speculation, psychological need, drug company promotion and political expediency had been fused with an evangelical fervor to produce what is undoubtedly the most powerful movement in — and beyond — contemporary education. (pp. 30–31)

Radical Sociological and Philosophical Foundations of Special Education

Radical critiques have not been prominent even on a small scale or attempted at all on a large scale within American special education.

Tomlinson (1982) did do a good broad radical critique in book format about British special education, *A sociology of special education*. Shapiro (1980) uses a radical analysis to examine one very narrow area which covers a small time frame on the historical development of American special education. Shapiro centered his paper on mainstreaming, or rather, its limitations. He wrote: 'The attempt at reform, in special education, or in any other areas of the field, becomes the attempt to resolve issues arising not simply out of education itself, but out of the broader social domain' (p. 223). Other American writers have tied implicitly the general culture to certain specific important aspects of special education: language, intelligence, classification or labeling, etc. None, until this work, *comprehensively* tie together major cultural factors (social, political, and economic) to the historical development of American special education.

It is surprising that there has been so little comprehensive philosophical and sociological work addressed to American special education of any kind because it has existed — since 1817 — for so long. Professional philosophers of education and sociologists of education have not really been very interested in special education. Although this is seemingly unfortunate, a functionalist approach, which has been the predominant social science paradigm for years, would merely have provided a rationale for what exists rather than what should be or why. *Philosophical perspectives in special education* by Kelly, an American, did not come out until 1971, while Tomlinson's *Sociology* (1982) is much newer. Let us look first at *Sociology*.

What has been produced to date, and on a wide scale, has been work on teaching methodology and curriculum — the latter encompassing the goals, aims, and objectives of special education. Much of the special education literature heretofore has been '. . . "practitioners talking to each other" — that is, the emphasis on what to do, rather than on any theoretical consideration as to why it is done' (Tomlinson, 1982, p. 134). Tomlinson believes that special school curriculum is the heart of a sociological analysis of special education, so she looked at the relationship of curriculum to social factors.

Tomlinson took up Young's (1971) challenge in analyzing the 'taken for granted curriculum', in a different area, special education. Any curriculum itself is comprised of certain knowledge, and Tomlinson put British special education in a 'new' sociological perspective. Tomlinson's thesis is that special educational curriculum — as with any type of education — is related to knowledge and power. She also points out that sociology has virtually no input into special educational policy or practices, and wrote her book 'to bring sociological perspectives to bear upon those social processes' and to show 'particularly the way in which people or groups exercise power and influence, and can shape and change special education' (p. 7).

Tomlinson who credits the idea for the passage below to Young (1971) and Bernstein (1975) wrote:

> It is a truism that every society makes different kinds and amounts of knowledge available to different categories of people and it has become a sociological truism that there are high- and low-status areas of knowledge, and that academic-type knowledge has a higher status than manual or manipulative skills. (p. 135)

The implication is that special education is a lower form of education because those prescribed it usually cannot succeed in ordinary education, and therefore they often become credential-deprived. This is despite the fact that 'part of the rhetoric of special needs includes the attempt to present whatever passes for special education as a benevolent "good" for individual children' (Tomlinson, 1982, p. 73).

There is also much disagreement about the extent to which the school age population is educationally handicapped, and therefore how many students should be served by special education. There are problems of definition to be sure among the special educators, but the actual numbers are really more a reflection of social factors and legislative decree. 'Those currently responsible for recommendations and legislation concerned with special education are implicitly, if not explicitly, aware that they are still largely dealing with the "social problem" class' (Tomlinson, 1982, p. 71).

Kelly's (1971) *Philosophical perspectives* purported to make:

> the first attempt in the literature to propose philosophical rationales capable of unifying special education as a discipline. In the elaboration of this philosophy, I have sought not only to cover rationales necessary to its development, but also to resolve contemporary issues and problems threatening to impair special education's disciplinary unity. (p. vii).

There is no reason to doubt the premise it was a first attempt, but regarding resolution of contemporary issues and problems it is questionable at best. Unfortunately, only the second and last chapters should be considered philosophical in nature; they are: 'A special educational epistemology' (originally titled 'Toward a comprehensive paradigm of special educational functions' as a journal article in 1969 in the *Journal of Special Education*) and 'Epilogue — toward an ethic in special education'. The other eight chapters are merely a nice overview of the cultural, programmatic, and psychological constituents of special education.

When introducing the epistemology chapter, Kelly discusses the difficulty of tying together (what he calls) 'the major special educational functions of research, diagnosis, therapy and administration-supervision' which are said to be 'all too often studied only as they relate to specific content areas' (p. 9). Kelly felt 'the basic purpose of special education is to provide therapeutic-instructional benefit' for exceptional children and 'within this context, therapy and instruction are regarded as the major functions of special education' (p. 9). Kelly saw the main problem preventing the field of special education from having a unifying paradigm as being the separation of functions from content. He tried to resolve this separation 'within a unified theoretical context'. Kelly sought agreement through a functional approach, literally and epistemologically.

Kelly's kind of philosophy is similar to that of many local school districts which gets drawn up, filed, and forgotten about so it can be said there exist rationales for their programs. These rationales are generally superficially conceived by an administrator merely to comply with some regulation, and when special programs change, this file-drawer type of philosophy gathers more dust and is not even up-dated. This sort of philosophy is public versus professional. Philosophy of special education has almost always been after the fact, has not been done by professional philosophers of education or by those with knowledge of professional-type philosophy of education, and has not been systematically thought out.

Special education as a field has a unique set of problems primarily resulting from a lack of unity and self-direction. 'Research and debate in special education continues to be dominated by psychologists, particularly those working at the prestigious institutes concerned with special education' writes Tomlinson (1982, p. 185) about the UK, but this is probably also true of the USA as well. Special educational programs are today preponderantly the product of legislation and governmental funding procedures, and some variation in program implementation occurs because school administrators do things differently. College professors instruct the special education teachers and support staff; e.g., learning disabilities consultants, school psychologists and social workers — the latter group of three comprise the 'multidisciplinary (child study) team'. There are a number of professional special educator and parent groups representing different — and in some cases the same — types of handicapped youngsters. These various groups tug at the field from many different sides resulting in a diffusion of goals, responsibilities, and outlooks. Children, especially many of the so-called mildly handicapped, are often pawns in the power struggles of these vested interest groups.

Organization

The first question of the study is, 'What are the historical roots of American special education?' Chapter 2 will address this question by explaining the development of major generic American special education programs, program restrictiveness, mainstreaming and their implications from a new, root perspective. The second question — 'What are the historical and social roots of the concept of LD?' — is addressed by Chapter 3 which traces LD's stages in a unique manner that deliberately includes sociological and ideological aspects. Chapter 4 looks at the question, 'What are the historical and social roots of the LD controversy and how would an RSA analyze it?' The fourth question — which is dealt with in the final chapter — asks, 'What are the implications of an RSA for American special education, the LD controversy, and future practice and policy?'

Historical Foundations of American Special Education: A New Interpretation of the Roots and Development

Introduction

This chapter asks the question: What are the historical roots of American special education? The three subchapters that follow will, in part, deal with this question. They are: (1) Overview (historical background on American education in general and special education in particular), (2) the least restrictive educational environment (and the concept of mainstreaming), and (3) the ramifications of mainstreaming.

Special education is a term which has traditionally signified a need for alternative means and/or methods of educating students who are physically handicapped, have sensory impairments, are nonconforming, or otherwise 'learning disabled' (LD). The main emphasis of this chapter is to show what preceded LD — the newest special education category — and in general, how and why the schooling configurations it uses took shape. A secondary theme of Chapter 2 is that with the current emphasis on mainstreaming, it initially appeared as though a significant phase in American education (special class segregation) might pass. More precisely, the mass segregation of atypical or exceptional or educationally handicapped children — which had reached its largest peak to date by the mid-1970s — seemed as though it could decline due to federal legislation of 1975. That is, the earlier established types of specially labeled children would now be integrated in greater numbers back into regular educational programs. However, the same federal statute (PL94–142), that in 1975 emphasized the right to be specially educated in the least restrictive environment, actually institutionalized the LD label on a large scale. (This will be elaborated in subsequent chapters.)

Overview

General Education

Between 1852 and 1918, all states passed compulsory educational attendance laws. Massachusetts was first and Mississippi, with a population that was more than 50 per cent black, was last (Cremin, 1961). The generally accepted reason that it took so long from the founding of the United States of America in 1776 until as late as 1918 for compulsory education is a lack of funding. Rippa (1980) — in referring to plans drafted by Thomas Jefferson between 1781 and 1825 to help educate the poor of Virginia — wrote: 'Indeed, in a society of class distinctions, the failure of the plan was undoubtedly caused by the refusal of well-to-do citizens to pay taxes for the education of the poor' (p. 70). The best even Jefferson could do was to see his efforts result in the opening of the University of Virginia in 1825 (the year before his death) which helped little to educate the general populace. So in addition to funding itself, there were also the issues of racism and social class. Prior to then, most education was conducted by the family, churches, private schools, or voluntarily supported municipal common schools, the predecessors of today's public schools (Curti, 1959). Horace Mann of Massachusetts and others, later convinced the affluent that educating the lower classes was in their best interests. Hoffman (1974) alleged that the real impetus for compulsory education was due to a mass influx of immigrants during the late 1800s and early 1900s who needed Americanization. Cremin (1961) goes a step further when he asserts that this wave of immigration was perceived as a threat to the Anglo-Teutonic order since so many emigrated from Eastern and Southern Europe. Teachers were delegated as the agents of their Americanization (Rippa, 1980).

Probably one of the most significant innovators in American public education was William Torrey Harris (1835–1909) who, while superintendent of the St. Louis Public Schools, incorporated the Kindergarten into his school system in 1873. Though Harris gained fame for many things — as the fourth US Commissioner of Education, for his editorship of the *Journal of Speculative Philosophy* and through his support for the founders of American philosophy, such as John Dewey (1930, 1981) — his primary legacy to American education is his development of the K-8-4 grade plan for school. This plan of grade placement and tracking became an important rationale for special education programs based on grade level achievement expectancies and comparison (i.e., test scores).

In this section it has been suggested that mass public general education (a) was reluctantly supported by the wealthy, (b) then began deliberately to serve American chauvinistic aims, (c) became institutionalized nationally, by 1918, through compulsory attendance laws, and (d) developed a basic format — the K-8-4 gradation. Special education, in some ways, has actually run a later, parallel course; and it was not until general education had become entrenched that special education could really develop. Only when the attitude prevailed that all children should attend school did education for the impaired receive much attention. It was then that accommodations and methods for the disabled were first studied seriously. More importantly, at that time, standards by which to judge an educational handicap were determined in conjunction with the requirements of regular education. In addition, these standards have become more refined, and as a result of this, special education has grown rapidly. Consequently, today, for those millions of students who display no physical or sensory impairment, failure to produce grade level academic work or the proper degree of behavioral conformity can lead easily to some form of special educational placement. This will become clearer by subsequent chapters. Let us now look at special education's beginnings.

Special Education

A pertinent question is: What happened to people before the appearance of special education of any kind? Hewett (1974) wrote that from man's earliest beginnings, individuals who were different have been destroyed, tortured, exorcised, sterilized, ignored, exiled, exploited, and even considered divine. Through most of recorded history, the mentally ill were not considered worthy of any education or training. They were, in fact, often locked up, chained, and/or put in straightjackets during the 1700s, 1800s, and later (Russell, 1941; Zilboorg and Henry, 1941). Pritchard (1963) discussed the superstitious attitude of 'divine displeasure' toward the physically handicapped and mentally retarded during the late 1700s. Also, Pritchard makes the cogent point that all forms of retardation were not noticeable at a time when few individuals could read and write, and that it was only when mass general education was widely accepted that the retarded stood out.

The earliest period of American special education was involved solely with institutionalization. The first special education school in America was The American Asylum For The Education And Instruction Of The Deaf established in 1817 at Hartford, Connecticut, by Reverend Thomas Gallaudet (Cruickshank, 1967). It is now known as the American School For The Deaf and is considered a fine school.

With the advent of compulsory education (1852 to 1918), many handicapped children were forced to attend school.

Educators in the public schools, unable to handle the exceptional children arriving in record numbers and realizing that no special provisions were available for these youngsters, began a movement for the establishment of special classes. Special classes came about, then, not for humanitarian reasons but because exceptional children were unwanted in the regular public school classroom. Feelings against mainstreaming, that is, placing exceptional children in regular classrooms, were strong. (Chaves, 1977, p. 30)

However, most children who were wheelchair-bound, not toilet trained, or considered uneducable were excluded because of the problems that schooling them would entail. It was not until after 1920 that educational programs for crippled children were organized in the form of decentralized hospital-school facilities, diagnostic centers, and local clinics (Cruickshank, 1967).

The next significant period in special education — after the 'institutionalization phase' — entails the formation of day schools, special classes, and public school involvement. This period began in the late 1800s and is still going on although more slowly (except for youngsters classified LD). The cities took the lead in establishing day schools and special classes for the handicapped within regular public schools (see Table 1). Robinson and Robinson (1965) detail the special class spiral between the first and second world wars:

From 1915 to 1930, the number of special classes in public day schools increased greatly, but from 1930 to 1940 there was a halt and even a decline in this trend. The financial burdens of the Depression, dissatisfaction with the premature establishment of inadequately planned special classes with untrained teachers, and misinterpretation of the assumptions of progressive education (typified by the notion that any basically good teacher could teach any group of children) combined to dampen public enthusiasm for special education. (p. 460)

As a result, most retarded children remained in regular classes, many attending school year after year without learning much (Cruickshank, 1967). However, after World War II: 'special classes were again promoted enthusiastically. A large impetus came from parents' groups, who combined forces to demand special facilities for their handicapped children' (Robinson and Robinson, 1965, p. 460).

In 1911 New Jersey was the first state to have compulsory special (education) class laws for the deaf, blind, and educationally retarded (New Jersey Commission, 1965). In 1954, NJ required local school districts to

Table 1: *Chronology of early milestones in American special eduation*

Year	Event
1817	The American Asylum For The Education And Instruction Of The Deaf And Dumb established at Hartford, Conn. by Reverend Thomas Gallaudet (Cruickshank, 1967) and became the first school in America to educate the handicapped. It is now known as the American School For The Deaf.
1829	The boarding school above became known as the American Asylum for the Deaf and Dumb and was the first place in America to provide education for the 'feebleminded' (Heck, 1940).
1929	The New England Asylum For The Blind founded. It became the Massachusetts School For The Blind in 1932; and later Perkins Institute in Watertown (Farrell, 1956).
1846	The first ever state supported educational facility for socially maladjusted was set up in Westborough, Massachusetts (Hoffman, 1974).
1848	The first institution established solely for the intellectually retarded (moderate) in America was a private residential school (The Experimental School For Teaching and Training Idiotic Children) in Barre, MA, founded by Dr. Hervey Wilbur (L'Abate and Curtis, 1975). The Commonwealth of Massachusetts in 1846 appropriated funds of $2500 per year for a three-year period for this school. It became known as The Massachusetts School of Idiotic and Feebleminded Youth in 1850 when the Commonwealth assumed full funding (Howe, 1858).
1858	American Printing House for the Blind founded in Louisville, Kentucky. It is a private publisher, and is the largest of its kind in the world today.
1864	National Deaf-Mute College was formed as the higher education division of Columbia Institution for the Instruction of the Deaf, Dumb, and Blind (founded in 1857), a residential school in Washington, District of Columbia (DC), the USA's capital city. Although private educational facilities, the US government began making contributions to both shortly after their establishment because: (a) Washington, DC is administered by the federal government as a unique 'municipality', and (b) their founders were influential. As of 1894, the higher division was called Gallaudet College. From its inception in 1864, it was and remains the world's only liberal arts college for the deaf.
1867	Federal Office of Education formed.
1868	The Horace Mann School in Roxbury, Mass., became the first (special educational) day school in the United States (Dunn, 1973; Heck, 1940).
1871	A day school for deaf pupils was established in Boston — becoming the first major city to do so (Dunn, 1973).
1876	Cleveland founded first day school for incorrigibles (Heck, 1940).
1892	Chicago established a special class for delinquents (Heck, 1940).
1896	Providence, RI, set up a class for the so-called Educable Mentally Retarded (Dunn, 1973).
1899	Chicago formed a class for crippled children (Dunn, 1973).
1900	Chicago set up the first day school for the educationally blind (Hathaway, 1966).
1907	Wisconsin became the first state to pass a day school law for the deaf (Heck, 1940).
1911	New Jersey became the first state in the nation to *mandate* the establishment of *special classes* — for the deaf, the blind, and the educationally retarded (L'Abate and Curtis, 1975; NJ Commission on The Education of the Handicapped, 1965).
1913	Roxbury, Mass., formed the first special class for the partially sighted (Hathaway, 1966).
1930	Section on Exceptional Children and Youth in the US Office of Education formed.
1954	NJ's first Beadleston Act *mandated* local school districts to identify and provide appropriate educational programs with state aid for physically handicapped and mentally retarded (trainable) pupils (NJ Commission, 1965).
1959	NJ's second Beadleston Act encouraged local school districts to provide educational services (expert consultation and financial reimbursement by the state to local districts) for emotionally disturbed and socially maladjusted children (NJ Comm., 1965).
1963	Section on Exceptional Children expanded to Division of Exceptional Children and Youth (see 1930, above).

Table 1—Continued

Year	Event
1964	NJ's Grossi Amendment (to the Beadleston Act of 1959) permitted local school boards to enter into a sending-receiving type relationship with nonsectarian, nonprofit private schools for emotionally disturbed and socially maladjusted children (NJ Comm., 1965).
1966	Bureau of Education for the Handicapped created within US Office of Education.
1975	The federal government of the United States of America passed The Education for All Handicapped Chidren Act which required all states to provide a free, appropriate education for all handicapped children and youth in the least restrictive (educational) environment.
1979	A separate Cabinet-level US Department of Education was formed (via PL96-88 'Department of Education Organization Act') to administer all programs that had been previously part of the US Department of Health, Education, and Welfare (HEW). This resulted in the creation of a US Office of Special Education and Rehabilitative Services (with a bureau called Special Education Programs) within the US Dept. of Education.

provide physically handicapped and retarded (trainable) students 'appropriate educational programs' (NJ Commission, 1965). With Montana passing special education laws in 1955, all states had special education statutes on the books — although some of it was permissive (noncompulsory), and some provided only partial reimbursement to the local school districts (Gilmore, 1956). There was an upsurge in special education funding by the states and the federal government after World War II, especially during the late 1950s and the 1960s (Reynolds, 1975). By the early 1960s special classes had attained nearly universal acceptance as a means for educating exceptional children (West and Bates, 1977).

Much of the federal legislation for the handicapped was passed between 1957 and 1967 (Chaves, 1977), but *none* of it dealt with least restrictive environments or compulsory attendance of handicapped students in local school systems (see Table 2).

Table 2:   Selected federal legislation related to the education of the handicapped (adapted from Davis, 1980; and public records)

Year	Act or Amendment
1867	An Act of Congress provided free entrance to the National Deaf-Mute College for a very limited number of poor deaf students from any US state or territory.
1879	Federal Act of 1879 'To Promote the Education of the Blind'. Since its enactment has provided annual appropriations to the American Printing House for the Blind for the manufacture of educational texts and aids, free of charge, for use by legally blind students of less than college level throughout the US and its possessions.
1956	PL85-531 'Cooperative Research Act'. Congress earmarked $667,000 for special education for the mentally retarded. First major and contemporary piece written for special education at the national level.
1958	PL85-905 'Captioned Films for the Deaf' funding.
1958	PL85-926 'Grants For Teaching In The Education Of Handicapped Children'. Money given to colleges and states to train with graduate fellowships teachers of the mentally retarded at $1,000,000 annually for 10 years. Very significant in that it is such a higher amount than ever previously appropriated for special education.

Table 2—Continued

Year	Act or Amendment
1959	Federal funding for professional preparation in institutions of higher learning (college professors) for training future teachers of the handicapped.
1961	PL87-276 Funds to colleges for a 3-year period for training teachers of the deaf, graduate and undergraduate levels.
1963	PL88-164 (amended PL85-926) 'Mental Retardation Facilities and Community Mental Health Center Construction Act'. Title III: 'Section 301' provided funds (student stipends and dependency allowances) for training personnel in all types and all levels of special education (including school supervisors and administrators). Free education was provided for graduate students, in the form of $2,500 support grants to colleges for each of their students, to work with types of handicapped children not covered by previous bills; e.g., the seriously emotionally disturbed, the visually handicapped, crippling conditions and other health impaired (this would include LD!), and for speech correctionists. Title III: 'Section 302' covered research and demonstration projects for handicapped.
1965	PL89-10 'Elementary and Secondary Education Act (ESEA) of 1965, As Amended'. 'Title I' of this act provided direct educational aid (funds) to states for compensatory education to socioeconomically deprived youngsters. Legally, they are not considered handicapped. (Title II covered books and materials, Title III education centers and services, Title IV research and training, and Title V strengthened state departments of education or State Education Agencies, SEAs.)
1965	PL89-36 Funds were provided for the first ever directly fully supported federal special educational facility: The National Technical Institute For The Deaf, at the Rochester Institute of Technology, for advanced vocational training.
1965	PL89-313 An amendment to 'Title I' of the 'Elementary and Secondary Education Act' (ESEA) to fund the education of handicapped children in state-operated or state-supported schools, such as institutions for the retarded. (PL89-313 further amended in 1975, allowed these funds to follow students moving from SEA programs to those in local districts. In 1977, an internal agreement within the US Office of Education, between Elementary and Secondary Education and Special Education, delegated all fiscal authority of such funds, except for the annual determination of these funds to the states, to Special Education).
1966	PL89-694 The Model Secondary School for the Deaf (MSSD), to be the second directly funded by US government at Gallaudet College in Washington, DC.
1966	PL89-750 (Morse-Carey amendment to PL89-10 became Title VI of ESEA.) 'Title VI' of ESEA which pertains to the education of handicapped children was passed. Included granting of direct aid to programs for handicapped children. It established the Bureau of Education for the Handicapped in Washington, DC with three divisions: research, educational services, and training programs, and the National Advisory Committee for the Handicapped.
1967	Amendments to Title VI set up regional resource centers for the deaf and blind. A tag of this amendment required that 15% of all Title II monies go for the handicapped.
1968	PL90-538 'Handicapped Children's Early Education Assistance Act'. Designed to establish experimental programs for young handicapped (preschools) that could serve as models for SEAs and local educational agencies (LEAs or local school districts) in the areas of practices and materials.
1969	'Children With Learning Disabilities Act of 1969' passed by the 91st Congress (as Bills S.1190 on February 28, 1969, and H.R.11310 on October 6, 1969) authorizing training, research, and service in LD. However, no appropriation made for these services then (see 1970, Title VI-G below, of which this act became a part).
1970	PL91-230 'Education of the Handicapped Act': 'Elementary and Secondary Education Amendments of 1969'. Title VI of the 1969 amendments combined into one act a number of previously isolated legislative enactments related to handicapped children, and was called the 'Education of the Handicapped Act'. Some of the new programs added to Title VI were the development of (1) Regional Resource Centers; (2) Centers and Services for Deaf–Blind Children; and (3) programs to serve children with specific learning disabilities.

Table 2—Continued

Year	Act or Amendment
	The most prominent funding effort started under Title VI-G (and later continued under PL94-142) was that which created the Child Service Demonstration Center (CSDC). There were 97 such centers in all during the time span within which the CSDCs operated, 1971 to 1980. Every state and the Commonwealth of Puerto Rico was served by at least one. While the average life span of any given CSDC was three years, a number persisted over additional years through multicycle funding. (Mann, Davis, Boyer, Metz, and Wolford, 1983, p. 14)
	The Bureau of Education for the Handicapped, through Title VI-G of PL91-230, has funded five research institutes in learning disabilities. These institutes are to: a) conduct research on the nature and educational treatment of children with specific learning disabilities, b) work directly with client populations, and c) produce a set of responsible educational interventions. The research institutes are located at the following universities: University of Illinois — Chicago, Columbia University — Teachers College, University of Kansas, University of Minnesota, and University of Virginia.
	During this first year of funding all institutes are involved in program planning and the refinement of their research missions. Programmatic research efforts will begin in the summer or fall of 1978 and will continue for as long as four years.
	The establishment of five major research institutes is a very significant step in the learning disability field. Historically, Title VI-G funds have focused primarily on the demonstration of existing research and practice through Child Service Demonstration Centers. The goal of these model centers over the past five years has been that of providing effective educational services and training, but through these efforts, many conceptual and educational concerns have surfaced. It has become clear that their resolution depends on intensive research efforts. The research institutes are directed to this end. (Deshler, 1978, p. 68)
	Title VI-G provisions of PL91-230 are formally known as 'Special Programs for Children with Specific Learning Disabilities'.
1970	PL91-517 'Developmental Disabilities Services And Construction Act of 1970'. Programs for neurological conditions related to mental retardation: cerebral palsy and epilepsy. First federal education support for this.
1970	PL91-587 Kendall Demonstration Elementary School for the deaf established at Gallaudet became the third school directly funded by the US government.
1972	PL92-424 'Economic Opportunity Amendments of 1972'. 10% of Head Start programs to be available for handicapped.
1973	PL93-112 'Rehabilitation Act of 1973'. 'Section 503' of this act required employers with federal contracts over $2500 to hire handicapped individuals. 'Section 504' of this act is like a bill of rights for the handicapped as it covered all ages and areas of life.
1974	PL93-247 'Child Abuse Prevention and Treatment Act'.
1974	PL93-380 'Education Amendments of 1974'. Extended ESEA of 1965 and laid the groundwork for PL94-142 of 1975 (by amending PL91-230). Reaffirmed rights of all children to an education without financial barriers, including the handicapped. PL93-380 also included the 'Family Rights and Privacy Act' (Title V, Secs. 513, 514), more commonly known as the 'Buckley Amendment' which allows one's review of own school records within 45 days of request.
1974	PL93-516 'Rehabilitation Act Amendments of 1974, Section IIIa' was enacted into law on December 7, 1974. It amended Section 504, which originally was essentially restricted to employment, and now included educational services.
1975	PL94-103 'Developmental Disabilities Assistance and Bill of Rights Act of 1975'. Amended PL91-517 of 1970 to include autism, and also dyslexia if it is attributable to the other specified developmental disabilities. It also guaranteed such right to attend school with nonhandicapped to the maximum extent possible, and test materials be non-discriminatory.
1975	PL94-142 'The Education for All Handicapped Act of 1975'. The most comprehensive and significant piece of legislation regarding the education of the handicapped. It is an amendment and extension of 'Part B of PL93-380'. It applies to all handicapped

Table 2—Continued

Year	Act or Amendment
	children and youths, ages 3–21 inclusive and denotes specific categories of impairment: deaf/hard of hearing, deaf–blind, mentally retarded, multihandicapped, orthopedically impaired, other health impaired, seriously emotionally disturbed, specific learning disability, speech-impaired, and visually handicapped. In brief, PL94-142 mandates a free, appropriate public education (FAPE) for all handicapped children and youths. Special education and related services must be provided at no cost to the child or one's parents. All handicapped children and their parents shall be guaranteed due process with regard to identification, evaluation, and placement procedures. A written individualized education program (IEP) must be developed and implemented for each child receiving special education services.
	Although PL94-142 was enacted on November 29, 1975, the provision concerning the IEPs for handicapped students already served was not made effective until October 1, 1977. Moreover, this Act required that a FAPE be available for all handicapped children age 3 to 18 by September 1, 1978, and age 3 to 21 by September 1, 1980, *except* for children age 3 to 5 and 18 to 21 in states where this requirement is inconsistent with state law or practice or a court order. PL93-380 in 1974 mandated programs for identifying and locating handicapped children at the state level, while in 1975 PL94-142 extended this requirement to LEAs.
1976	PL94-482 'The Vocational Education Act Amendments of 1976'. Ten per cent of all state monies from federal funding to be used for vocational training of handicapped individuals of any age.
1978	PL95-602 'Rehabilitation, Comprehensive Services, and Developmental Disabilities Act'. Extends previous developmental disabilities to include tuberous sclerosis, osteogenesis imperfecta, and several others that occur during developmental years; i.e., before age 22.
1978	PL95-561 'Gifted and Talented Children's Education Act of 1978, Educational Amendment of 1978' (Title IX-A). Encouraged states to meet the needs of these children via funding.
1981	PL97-35 'Education Consolidation and Improvement Act of 1981, Title VI — Human Services Programs, Subtitle A, Chapter 4 (Section 605) — Other Handicapped Programs and Services'. Consolidated, in one chapter, annual funding, for fiscal years 1982–1984, to: a) the American Printing House for the Blind ($5,000,000), b) Gallaudet College, Kendall School, and MSSD ($52,000,000), and c) National Technical Institute for the Deaf in Rochester, NY ($26,300,000).
1983	PL98-199 'Education of the Handicapped Act Amendments of 1983'. *Mandated* in all states education for the handicapped ages 18 to 21 in the least restrictive environment.
1986	PL99-457 'Education of the Handicapped Act Amendments of 1986'. This reauthorization of PL94-142 provided increased funding, *mandated* in all states programs for the 'preschool handicapped' (ages 3 to 5), gave seed money for early intervention programs (birth to 3 years), and encouraged exploration of noncategorical alternatives.

Note: Civil rights legislation for handicapped students was given impetus by litigation.

The current phase of the history of special education, which this writer refers to as the 'desegregation phase', began in the 1960s. It began when influential persons started to look again into the efficacy of self-contained (segregated) special educational classes. It is perhaps an article by Burton Blatt that may have been the first in a professional journal of this era to trigger off this far-reaching controversy ('Some persistently recurring assumptions concerning the mentally subnormal', 1960). Blatt questioned the benefits of special classes and found few significant differences between handicapped children in special classes and those in regular ones. Landmark articles by G. Orville Johnson: 'Special education for the mentally handicapped — A paradox' (1962), and Lloyd M. Dunn: 'Special education for the mildly retarded — Is much of it justifiable?' (1968), followed Blatt, causing many professional educators as well as concerned others to re-think educational policy regarding the handicapped. Some other similar but less well known publications from the middle to later 1960s are by Goldstein, Moss, and Jordan (1965); Hoeltke (1966); Rubin, Simson, and Betwee (1966); plus Smith and Kennedy (1967). Other professional literature in this area was subsequently generated in the 1970s, e.g., Nelson and Schmidt (1970), Filler *et al.*, (1975), among others — and still is into the 1980s.

The 1960s and early 1970s had set the stage for the passage of important national legislative bills in the mid-1970s. One act required that all states provide all educationally handicapped students free programs, while the other required that the program provided be the least restrictive environment possible (see Table 2).

Least Restrictive Educational Environment

It was shown in the first subchapter that education for the handicapped, or lack of it, progressed through several distinct periods or phases. Reynolds (1975) discussed special education as having five 'progressive inclusion' stages. (1) Prior to 1850 handicapped individuals were abused or neglected but not educated. (2) From around 1850 to 1900 residential schools were provided for education and training. (3) From approximately 1900 to 1950 special schools and special classes became more prevalent while residential schools continued to grow and expand. (4) During the 1950s and 1960s special classes became the preferred type of educational service for students with mild cognitive impairments, while residential institutions and special schools flourished for the blind, deaf, and physically handicapped. (5) From about 1970 onward placement in regular classes of handicapped students who are able to be socially and instructionally integrated occurred. Development of special classes in regular public schools for some handicapped students formerly placed in residential institutions and special day schools has also taken place. This author refers to Reynolds' stage two as the 'institutionalization phase', his third and fourth stages as the 'special class/ day school phase', and his fifth stage as the 'desegregation phase'. Dunn's (1973) relevant statement is quoted here: 'With today's emphasis on respect for the individual, the practice of segregating children with learning disabilities into self-contained special education programs is about to be markedly reduced' (p. 52). In fact, there is even a movement to do away with the handicapping categories or labels and merely address the educational problems or characteristics. For instance, mental retardation becomes cognitive disadvantage, orthopedically handicapped becomes physical disadvantage, a speech deficit or a learning disability becomes communicative disadvantage, vision or hearing problems are sensory disadvantages, and emotional disturbance or behavioral disorder becomes emotional/behavioral disadvantage (Turnbull and Schulz, 1979).

Mainstreaming is the educational arrangement of placing handicapped students in regular classes with their nonhandicapped peers to the maximum extent appropriate (Turnbull and Schulz, 1979). The degree to which a handicapped student can be mainstreamed should be determined by the need of the student, not by what the school system presently has to offer (as per PL94–142). A list of all possible needs would be rather extensive, some are: academic remediation, social skills training, auditory training, various types of perceptual motor exercises, speech correction, language development, physical therapy, occupational therapy, adaptive physical education, low pupil-teacher ratio for all or part of the school day, a stress-free milieu, transportation to and from school, a barrier-free environment, educational counselling and so forth. Goals and objectives should be planned as part of the development of an Individual Educational Program (IEP; see PL94–142 in Table 2). Then, the program providing the most normal type of setting is to be implemented. When all of this has been done for the handicapped pupil, he/she is considered properly mainstreamed or in the least restrictive (educational) environment possible.

The notion of least restrictive environment refers to the type of program the handicapped student is placed into and the ancillary special educational services to help maintain it. Reynolds (1962) provided a framework for special education programming, Deno (1970) offered a cascade model of special educational services, and Dunn (1973) supplied an inverted pyramid to display eleven major administrative special education plans with decreasing normalization going toward the small end at the bottom. This author has devised a similar one as shown in Table 3, following.

Ramifications of Mainstreaming

When children who are difficult to educate are segregated, they not only lose opportunities otherwise afforded the general school population, such as diversification of academic courses and extracurricular activities; but they also are deprived of an environment for normal psychosocial development.

Table 3:   Hierarchy of less increasingly restrictive educational programs

  1.   Total Mainstreaming (No Special Educational Services)
  2.   Individualized Program In Regular Class*
  3.   Regular Class Attendance Plus Supplemental Instruction for one period per day:
                (a) Individual (b) Group
  4.   Resource Room for 2 or 3 periods per day
  5.   Special Class in Home School District
  6.   Special Class out of Home School District
  7.   Special Public School
  8.   Special Private School
  9.   Special Residential School
 10.   Hospital-Based Schooling
 11.   Home Instruction

Variations are possible for numbers 2 through 11.

It should be noted that program restrictiveness may have to be altered as the child progresses through school and requires a change depending on the progress made.

In this regard Beery (1972) writes about 'physical, administrative and psychological distance'. According to Cruickshank (1967) the concept of classification — the labeling of educationally handicapped students — took hold between 1920 and 1930. Guskin and Guskin (1970) discuss the concept of 'socially induced deviance' and labeling.

> Once you have been identified as different, others define a new role for you; they expect different things from you and place different demands on you, which in turn is likely to alter your behavior so that you fit the role, i.e., your behavior resembles the expectations more closely. (p. 95)

Academic gains are also impeded. Rosenthal and Jacobson (1968) showed how teachers do not expect or push for much academic performance from their students who are thought to be dull, even if they are not. Guskin and Guskin (1970) also discussed the negative effects of differential treatment.

> The case of the institutionalized deviate may be more dramatic than the way in which deviates are treated in the community and in public schools, but it is a difference in degree and not in kind. Deviant roles and role expectations are also created for the mentally retarded and problem child in the public schools, both in segregated classes and within the regular classes. In what seems at first to be a beneficial situation, a child thought to be retarded may be given less challenging tasks by the teacher. While this protects the child from failure, it may reduce his opportunity to learn. (p. 95)

So while less achievement is sought from labeled and/or segregated students, it becomes that much more difficult for them to get back into regular educational programming. As was pointed out earlier, relative improvement comparison through testing is the key to returning to more or all of a normalized schedule, but the path is often quite difficult.

Although the thrust of the mainstreaming movement is geared toward getting the mildly educationally handicapped back into a more normal setting, this movement can provide beneficial effects for the more severely impaired. For instance, take the case of a regular Kindergarten through eighth grade public school which houses classes for both the educable mentally retarded (EMR or mildly retarded IQ range generally from 50 to 69) as well as trainable mentally retarded (TMR or severely to moderately retarded IQ range generally 25 to 50). Many EMRs could be mainstreamed with same-aged peers for most non-academic subjects such as gym, shop, or art; while the very mildly EMR pupils might be able to participate with same-aged peers or those slightly their junior in the regular classroom for academics. This, of course, is assuming that the mildly retarded could not, for quite valid reasons, be totally mainstreamed or work out of a resource room. In addition, the higher functioning TMRs could be given the chance to participate with the slower EMR reading groups or in some of their other activities. This cannot happen when TMR youngsters are required to attend a segregated regional special TMR school. It seems as though the profoundly retarded (IQ below 25) who are often multiply handicapped physically as well, will continue to be kept out of the public schools and remain at hospital affiliated centers and special day or residential schools because they cannot benefit from mainstreaming at a public school — in addition to other complex psychosocial and economic reasons.

At the other end of the schooling spectrum, the handicapped are attending college in greater numbers. As their specific needs are being recognized, it could be said that even college students are being mainstreamed. There are:

> expanding opportunities in higher education for most of the disabled, especially those confined to wheelchairs and those with visual or hearing impairments. Since Section 504 of the Vocational Rehabilitation Act of 1973 prohibits discrimination against the handicapped at institutions receiving Federal funds, administrators have been scrambling to open campus buildings and programs to the disabled. In addition, the Education of All Handicapped Children Act of 1975, also known as Public Law 94–142, requires that public schools 'mainstream' these students, placing them in regular classes to the greatest extent possible. The law has subsequently opened up college-preparatory programs to students previously placed in special-education or lower-level classes and

effectively precluded them from attending college. (Winslow, 1982, p. 87)

Another problem that must be faced when mainstreaming is attempted is resistance from those responsible for carrying it out: teachers and principals. After being conditioned to believe that deviant or handicapped students should be separated out of regular classes, principals and especially teachers believe that these exceptional students are being 'dumped back on them' without adequate preparation, training, or assistance.

It must be borne in mind that not all of those jumping on the mainstreaming bandwagon are doing so for solely egalitarian reasons. The total per capita annual expenditure is considerably less for a nonclassified student, and in this sense, mainstreaming saves money. So in this political era of fiscal austerity, the concept of mainstreaming is welcomed by many.

Perhaps the most important social ramification of the wholesale implementation of mainstreaming lies within the realm of minority enrollment in classes for the mildly retarded. There is a disproportionate over-representation of ethnic minorities found in these classes (Beery, 1972; Larry P. v. Riles, 1979; Manni, Winikur and Keller, 1980), primarily Afro-Americans, American-Indians, Mexican-Americans, and Puerto Rican-Americans. Selection of students for these classes has been recently changed and more who formerly would have been placed in classes for the Educable Mentally Retarded remain in the mainstream (or get placed in LD programs).

An important outcome that this writer sees as inevitable because of the mainstreaming movement is that of extensive 'tracking'. This was commonly done prior to the largescale advent of special classes (Harap, 1936), and was variously called 'sorting', 'multi-tracking', and 'streaming'. Tracking is really just ability grouping.

> By relegating the less able and the nonconforming into the lower track, educators found a way of setting such children aside. And it must be recognized that a self-contained special class is just another name for this lower track. . . . From more recent U.S. studies, it would appear that homogeneous grouping works to the disadvantage of slower children in most of today's schools. . . . Conversely, homogeneous grouping works to the advantage of more able students. (Dunn, 1973, pp. 45–46)

The philosophical issue of whether the brightest should be separated and for how much from the others becomes apparent here again in another form, but is beyond the scope of this work. It is not uncommon today for large school districts to have what this writer calls 'educational layers' or tracks operating simultaneously with some being publicized while others are not. The following list, in order of descending academic challenge, is used for illustrative purposes with 'NP' indicating that a layer is not publicized: intellectually gifted, honors or 'star' classes, regular college prep, vocational training, general education, 'C' or slow learner classes (NP), 'trouble-makers' (NP), Educable Mentally Retarded, and Trainable Mentally Retarded. (This list does not include classes for handicapped whose primary classifications are emotionally disturbed or learning disabled since classes of those types are theoretically set up for students who are of approximately average intelligence or potential). This author is specifically suggesting that many of the handicapped now in special education will be placed into non-publicized layers, with most of the mildly retarded in the slow learner or LD classes and the emotionally disturbed in the 'troublemaker' track. Resource room placement for two or three periods a day as a buffer or holding pattern is the only viable alternative to special classes or 'C-tracking', but this is still a type of track in itself.

Despite the foreseeable end to the very costly process of professional multidisciplinary team evaluation (which is required before a child can be officially labeled as being educationally handicapped and put in a special class), and the quite expensive maintenance of a special class apparatus for mildly handicapped youngsters of all types, a more subtle form of grouping slow learners and nonconformists could take its place. When this happens, the tracking cycle will have gone full swing, leaving behind the skeleton of a special education dinosaur that tried but failed to better educate the mildly handicapped in their own separate classes during a period when money was still available to do this. It is hoped that the rich remnants that are to be left behind will be better facilities for students with the lower incidence handicaps (the more severely handicapped youngsters) and a student's right not to be unnecessarily labeled or segregated.

Summary

This chapter was designed to answer the question pertaining to the origins of American special education's roots. We found, among other things, that except for very isolated instances where residential institutions for the severely handicapped were established, there was virtually no formal special education in the United States until the last quarter of the nineteenth century. The first residential school was founded in Connecticut during 1817, but most were not established until the second half of the nineteenth century. This writer calls the period from 1850 to 1900 the institutional-ization phase of American special education.

Though compulsory mass public education in the USA acts, by and large, as a means of conserving culture, its beginnings were related to social class and racial struggles. The wealthy did not want to pay for free public education. All the states did pass compulsory education laws between 1852 and 1918 — Mississippi, with a population of over 50 per cent black, was last.

When schooling became compulsory, accommodations had to be made for exceptional children as well. So contrary to popular belief today, special education did not come about for solely egalitarian and humane reasons. The major cities led the way in forming new schooling arrangements in what this author refers to as the special class/day school phase, circa 1900–1969. New Jersey in 1911 was the first state to *mandate* special classes for the deaf, blind, and educationally retarded (EMR). All states had special education statutes by 1955, but some of it was permissive (noncompulsory) and/or provided only partial reimbursement to local school districts.

The period from approximately 1970 to the present is referred to here as the desegregation phase. This latter phase characterizes the discontent over the growing amount of special class placements; and it actually began with the disproportionate make-up, primarily of minorities and the poor, in classes for the so-called educable mentally retarded. As a result of such growing negative sentiment for this sort of disproportionate placement and concomitant litigation, the most monumental piece of special education legislation was passed by the federal government, 'The Education for All Handicapped Act of 1975' (PL94–142). It guaranteed a free education to all handicapped students in the least restrictive environment.

The federal government formally became involved in special education with legislation beginning in 1957, and its role was really limited to research, training, and demonstration centers until the late 1970s. With the implementation of PL94–142 on October 1 1977, the federal government began paying for much of special education — including LD, which was one of 94–142's ten reimbursable categories. Special education has become a massive, formal mode in the longstanding school practice of tracking.

Chapter 3

The Evolution of Learning Disabilities:
An Analysis of the Roots of a Concept

In the histories of special education and the psychology of disability no issue has so suddenly captured the interest of parents, educators, pediatricians, psychologists, and the representatives of many other disciplines as has that generally termed 'learning disabilities'.
Daniel P. Hallahan and William M. Cruickshank (1973, p. ix)

Introduction

This chapter asks the question, What are the historical and social roots of the concept of learning disabilities (LD)? To answer this question, root cultural influences are included in addition to mere descriptive historical 'facts'. It is strongly believed that only in this way can real objectivity be approached. The prior functional descriptions properly traced 'what' happened during LD's evolution and 'how' the vectors of professional interest converged at its inception and afterwards. By contrast, the radical perspective here looks at 'why' LD developed as it did and the social purposes it served upon becoming institutionalized.

Previous accounts of the origins of learning disabilities can be faulted because they omitted the cultural groundwork which allowed the LD label to come into existence. They failed to include, strongly enough or at all, sociological and/or ideological factors. Examples of the previous type follow: Kirk and Gallagher's (1979) is brief but very well done for a small part of a textbook; Schmid's (1979) is a good general history with legislation and litigation, and Wiederholt's (1974) is the most scholarly and comprehensive LD history of this kind ever done. Such accounts are to some extent functional delusions whereby the resulting dominant practice and thought are justified by the outcome. These accounts are not done with nefarious intent. On the contrary, they were done with the purpose of being objective and providing historical information, but they did omit, deliberately or not and to varying degrees, cultural aspects. This is not to say that the functionalist writers did not believe in the dominant ideas, as they probably did. Yet even if they did not, their published work followed its accepted form, i.e., being functional, empirical, quantitative, and artificially objective. In this present account, the opposite tack is taken.

Wiederholt (1974) tied the diffuse LD field together well historically in a purely descriptive manner by conceptualizing it along two dimensions: a 'developmental-phase dimension' with three vertical 'subphases' and a three part horizontal 'disorder dimension'. Along the lateral disorder dimension, Wiederholt lists 'disorders of spoken language' (listening and speaking), 'disorders of written language' (reading and writing), and 'disorders of perceptual and motor processes' — which Myers and Hammill (1982), in their adaptation of Wiederholt, refer to as 'correlative disorders: perceptual-motor processes, hyperactivity-distractibility' (p. 21). As the LD field is so all-encompassing, few, including this writer, would argue about Wiederholt's characterization of the disorder dimension. What can be argued and will be done differently here, is the manner of presentation of the field's (vertical) historical development — this is the heart of the 'root' analysis.

The developmental dimension, to Wiederholt, is based on historical time and consists of three subphases: the 'foundation phase' ('circa 1800–1930'), the 'transition phase' ('circa 1921–1960'), and the 'integration phase' ('circa 1960–1970'). He wrote that his newest phase, which begins in 1960, 'cannot . . . be historical' (p. 141) because he felt it was too 'current'. Therefore, his account as well as even other more recent ones, is dated. (The significant growth in the creation of LD programs only within the past few years and important divergent thought regarding this practice will be addressed in detail within the next chapter.)

It is the current writer's opinion that Wiederholt's developmental phases for LD are, from the earliest onward, equivalent to overlapping periods that basically involve, more parsimoniously: (1) The 'pioneering medical contribution stage' (circa 1800–1950), primarily involving neurologists; (2) the 'remediation stage' (circa 1920–1962), whereby the earliest educational support-type staff members (reading, remedial reading, speech and audiology specialists in addition to psychologists) contributed; and (3) the birth of the relatively recent 'modern LD stage' (1962 to the present), made up of research-educators, special education teachers and administrators, as well as physical and occupational therapists plus formalized child study teams. This tripartite schema is utilized instead of Wiederholt's because it more easily reveals the professional disciplines involved, it is felt to be a better historical demarcation, and only with this format can very recent developments be addressed. However, in addition to those three basically descriptive and sequential stages, two other concurrent periods helped to bring about the modern LD stage and add much more to our cultural understanding of it: the 'child study movement' (1882 to the present) and the 'slow learner period' (circa 1935–1977).

When any complex concept is traced back in an attempt to discover its precursory origins a particular point of explanatory departure must be chosen to begin the journey. This point is therefore always arbitrary and open to much debate. For this work as a whole — which attempts to discover how the concept of learning disabilities evolved and why it ultimately became entrenched within American education — four overlapping essential precursors will be discussed. In order of presentation, they are: (1) the origins of the child study movement, (2) the pioneering medical contribution stage, (3) the remediation stage, and (4) the slow learner period. After the precursors, the modern LD stage will be addressed by the following four subchapters: the initial establishment of the LD label as a clinical entity, institutionalization of LD as an educational arrangement, contemporary practice, and the newer practice model.

Essential Precursors

The Origins of the Child Study Movement

G. Stanley Hall has come to be known as the father of the child study movement in the United States. 'As early as 1882, when he established his laboratory at Johns Hopkins, Hall decided to concentrate his energies on the hitherto unexplored problem of child development' (Cremin, 1961, p. 102). His monograph 'The contents of children's minds' (1883), based on questionnaire data, was his first contribution to receive widespread attention.

> His explicit conclusion there was that with the coming of cities, and the consequent changes in the experience of childhood, schools could no longer assume that children brought with them the same concepts as in the older farm days. But beneath this conclusion lay notions much more radical than the argument that subject matter might be taught more effectively if the results of child study were used. For Hall was really urging that the content of the curriculum could itself be determined from the data of child development. (Cremin, 1961, pp. 102–103)

This becomes more manifest in Hall's later articles such as 'Child-study and its relation to education' (1900) and 'The ideal school as based on child study' (1901–2). In the later piece he distinguishes between the 'scholiocentric' and the 'pedocentric' school, the former term being the previous dominant ideal of Western educational thought whereby the child fitted the school, while the latter is the opposite. Turning again to Cremin (1961), with Hall leading the way for a 'new emphasis on the scientific study of feelings, dispositions and attitudes as elements' in education, this 'shift was truly Copernican, its effects, legion' (p. 104). What Cremin means by this is that previously barred academic studies as well as reformers of all kinds (including feminists seeking emancipation via education), 'sentimentalists' ('the needs of children'), in addition to social scientists, would develop more interest in schools.

Hall assumed the presidency of Clark University in 1889 and continued to lecture there indefatigably where two of his more well known students were Lewis M. Terman (1877–1956) and Arnold Gesell (1880–1961). Terman is recognized for his work on IQ tests while Gesell is synonymous with maturational developmental scales. Gesell popularized the concept of maturation as the basis for development, and devised 'scales of development, for infants and pre-school children based on normative data of children from the Yale Clinic of Child Development' (Wolman, 1973, p. 159). Terman, in his initial 1916 English revision of the French language Binet-Simon intelligence test (which used Mental Age or MA, but not IQ), popularized the concept of IQ on his redesigned and standardized version which was named the Stanford-Binet Intelligence Scale. Hall also gained notoriety for arranging Sigmund Freud's visit to America in 1909. Hall is of great significance in establishing a place for psychology in the schools and for helping to legitimate the routine but 'scientific' study of differences among children within American schools. Hall, indirectly, aided the institutionalization of special education in America.

It cannot be emphasized strongly enough, that on the basis of these studied differences, rationales are promulgated for various educational programs, e.g., special education. Further, the state of New Jersey today requires a multidisciplinary group of three persons actually called a 'Child Study Team' — other states use similar names — to determine after referral, generally by a teacher, the eligibility of a child for special education. If eligible, which is usually the outcome, the Team determines the educationally handicapping condition and assigns the child one of several predesignated labels (categorically). It then recommends a suitable specialized program in a regular school or an appropriate special school. It must be noted, however, that not all states (such as Florida) require formal child study or multidisciplinary teams (MDTs); and in such states, the school psychologist has, with assistance from various other school staff, the primary and almost unilateral decision-making responsibility. Also, in various states (such as Massachusetts), special education students are classified and grouped noncategorically (without a formal clinical label) by handicapping condition, e.g., a speech deficit or a learning disability would be called a 'communicative disadvantage' (see, in this work, 'Least restrictive educational environment' subchapter of Chapter 2; and also Turnbull and Schulz, 1979). Nevertheless, regardless of whether full MDTs and/or clinical labels are utilized, the outcome for special education students today really remains the same, and this practice can be traced back to Hall's influence.

The Pioneering Medical Contribution Stage

It was demonstrated earlier how child study became normative practice primarily through the influence of the psychologist Hall and his students around the turn of the 20th century. What follows will point out how the field of medicine (primarily through the specialties of neurology, but also to some extent ophthalmology) helped advance thought on neurologically based learning problems from around 1800 to 1950. The major concern, initially, was actually with adults who had acquired brain damage or had strokes, their symptoms, and their readjustment or re-learning. 'The clinical observations of physicians were the primary bases on which these theories were built, and there was little or no empirical hypothesis testing using controlled research procedures' (Myers and Hammill, 1982, p. 20).

If it is felt that the true nature of LD is involved with communication/symbol problems and their associative neurological causes, as this writer does, then we can begin, from the earliest documented period, when around 3000 BC the Egyptians noted a concern for a loss of speech in conjunction with head injury (Schuell, Jenkins and Jiminez-Pabon, 1964). The study of the nature of physical injury is within the province of physicians, and disorders of the brain are naturally of interest to (physician) neurologists. However, according to Wiederholt (1974), 'it was not until the nineteenth century that hypotheses began to be posited regarding the specific causes of these disorders and descriptions recorded of patients with dysfunctions of speech and language' (p. 107). Therefore, Wiederholt began his formal history of LD in 1802 with a published letter by Franz Joseph Gall, who was a physician from Vienna. Gall believed that head injuries could result in disorders of mental ability which were associated with certain parts of the brain. (As important as Gall was to early modern medical science, he was later to be called a 'charlatan' because of his 'science of phrenology'). Gall examined a number of adults who sustained head injuries to the brain stem and lost speech, and he then conjectured this type of injury as causative (see Gall, 1807).

It is the contention here that the learning disabilities (LD) field has its historical roots in the study of aphasia. There are many specific types of aphasia, but perhaps the best general definition of aphasia is the 'Loss of or impaired ability to speak, write, or to understand the meaning of words, due to brain damage' (Wolman, 1973, p. 29). When we compare this general definition of aphasia with the earliest LD definition (found in Kirk, 1962; and Kirk and Bateman, 1962 — which are virtually identical), it is seen that the latter is merely an embellishment of the former. Myers and Hammill (1982) are of similar opinion.

> When one compares the current definition of learning disability with the observations of Gall, it is apparent that he was studying a condition (aphasia) that, if it occurred during childhood rather than in the adult, we today would call a specific language disorder and would categorize further as a learning disability. For further evidence of this, consider Gall's diagnostic procedures in light of our present-day definition. First, he noted that some of his patients could not speak but could write their thoughts proficiently, thus demonstrating the presence of intraindividual, that is, specific differences. Second, by documenting that the individual had been normal in verbal expression abilities prior to the head injury, he demonstrated that the problem definitely was a consequence of brain involvement (that is, damage, disorganization, or dysfunction) and that this physical impairment had in some way disrupted the functioning of those particular psychoneurological processes that permitted the accurate transmission of language through speech; that is, the presence of intrinsic deficits was confirmed. Third, he felt that it was critical to show that the patient's performance was not caused by other conditions, notably mental retardation or deafness. (p. 22)

To further accentuate the point about the historical relationship of LD to aphasia, Wiederholt, after having begun his earliest formal LD history with Gall, lists seven other European physicians who also studied spoken language disorders. All seven could be characterized as neurologists because of the focus of their work, and they further advanced the study of aphasia. (Wiederholt's information about them is from Head, 1926; and Schuell *et al.*, 1964.) The seven, with year of accomplishment or publication and country, are as follows. John Baptiste Bouillaud (1825, France) speculated from post-mortem examination that disorders of movement and sensation were due to difficulties in particular areas of the brain. Paul Broca (1861 a, 1861 b, France) postulated from autopsies that left brain functions were different than right, and speech disorders were localized to a particular brain area (third frontal convolution). John Hughlings Jackson (1874, England) followed Broca's lead about left side brain differences and tried to localize speech disorders in the cerebral cortex. During the debate over causes of aphasia, some Germans and Englishmen designed schemata (models) to explain language functions and were called by Head (1926) the 'diagram makers'. (Wiederholt, 1974, wrote that there are many diagram makers in the LD field today). Bastian and Wernicke were two of the most noted diagram makers. Henry Charlton Bastian (1887, England) believed speech disorders resulted from damage to visual or auditory brain centers or connecting neural motoric pathways required for speech such as lips or tongue or even the hand for writing. Carl Wernicke (1874, Germany) believed various brain parts served different functions, and damage to neural tracts attaching the auditory and the motor speech brain areas caused one of four types of aphasia: motor, conduction, sensory (later to be called Wernicke's aphasia), and total. Pierre Marie's (1906, France) theory was that internal speech could be intact but getting the words out ('exteriorization of language', Head, 1926, p. 68) was faulty, which produced what Marie called 'anarthria'. Henry Head (1926, England) did clinical assessment of World War I brain damaged patients, and stressed an integrated notion of language dysfunction, rejected notions of defects of intelligence for these patients, and opposed motor (expressive) versus sensory (receptive) classification of language disorders.

It was a coincidental set of circumstances — advances in European neurology, primarily aphasia, and the occurrence of World War I, which took place in Europe — that produced an unprecedented and hastened understanding of the behavioral manifestations of brain damage. It must be noted though, that the fortuitous medical advances as a result of the World War I era were at the cost of millions of casualties to perverse imperialist ideologies and ethnocentric chauvinism. Both Head and Kurt Goldstein (1878–1956) became famous for their work with the war victims.

Kurt Goldstein's research with brain damaged soldiers in Frankfurt am Main, Germany (see, for perhaps the best example in English, Goldstein, 1942), shortly after World War I, is another essential and most important specific precursor. Goldstein studied the after-effects of brain injuries sustained by German soldiers (Ross, 1977). He discovered a number of significant behavioral attributes of his soldiers with brain insult. 'Goldstein thus presented a picture of the severely brain-damaged adult as one who is stimulus bound, unable to deal with abstractions, incapable of differentiating between figure and ground, prone to catastrophic reactions, perseverative, meticulous, and orderly' (Ross, 1977, p. 19). Goldstein is usually cited when pointing up the problem a formerly normal, brain damaged (BD) adult has in using imagination and switching to different solutions to solve problems.

Pathological repetitiveness is known as perseveration and the inability to imagine a novel solution is what Goldstein called the absence of the 'abstract attitude'. His BD soldier would be able to drink water from a glass on request, but might be unable and puzzled at a similar request for a demonstration with an empty glass. This latter inability leads to frustration and the possible catastrophic emotional reaction; and therefore often the strong need for meticulous behavior to create an orderly environment to avoid possible future frustration due to more required novel problem solving or location tasks. Location problems relate to difficulty in the differentiation of figure (an object) from ground (the background). Goldstein was influenced by the Gestalt school of psychology which was popular at the time and was especially involved with the figure ground concept. A visual figure ground problem might involve locating an object embedded within a picture background or auditorily reproducing a rhythm — the pauses or silences representing background. Related to all this is the concept of being stimulus bound. If the BD soldier is presented with a number of colored buttons of different sizes and asked to sort them by some similar attribute, he could perhaps group them by color. Yet when asked to group them in another, related way, by size for instance, he might be unable to do this. There is an inability to shift strategies, and he remains bound or captive to the original stimulus utilized.

In addition to the work about brain damage on speech aphasia and perceptual-motor processes (the latter primarily by Goldstein and the former mainly by Gall and the previously named seven others after him), other physicians were working in an area then generally called alexia. Alexia is:

> Also called word blindness and visual aphasia. A form of aphasia in which there is an absence of the ability to grasp meaning from or to read the written or printed language. This condition is the result of organic brain damage and does not involve any impairment in vision or intelligence. The loss of a previous ability to read is called acquired alexia. If the condition involves an inability to learn to read that is not consistent with the individual's mental age and other intellectual achievements, it is referred to as congenital alexia. (Wolman, 1973, p. 18)

Geschwind (1962) wrote that one of the first physicians to report an 'acquired reading disability' was J. Dejerine of France in 1887. The earliest known pieces of literature in the English language dealing with the problem of reading disability were written almost simultaneously and published in England within a year of each other. They were penned by the physician James Kerr (1897) and the ophthalmologist W. Pringle Morgan (1896) —

the latter being more well known for his use of the phrase 'word-blindness' in print. Both pieces were about 'children who seemed to be intellectually normal . . . having difficulty learning to read' (Kaluger and Kolson, 1969, p. 54). Later, James Hinshelwood (1917), a physician based at the Glasgow Western Medical School — while in Mentone, France — first scientifically described 'congenital word blindness', (but he credited the German, Kussmaul, 1877, who named *aphasic* 'wortblindheit'). It has been written (see Herman, 1959; and Kaluger and Kolson, 1969) that C.J. Thomas (1905) and Hinshelwood (1917) both suggested congenital word-blindness was familial and hereditary. Hinshelwood 'was among the first to assert that some kinds of congenital brain defects might cause children to have developmental reading problems, . . . and to speculate about methods by which affected children could be taught to read' (Myers and Hammill, 1982, p. 22).

The last few physicians above, our alexia group, helped pave the way for the remediation stage to emerge. They also laid the groundwork for future work in dyslexia or reading dysfunctions — as contrasted with alexia, which is total inability to read. The neurologist S.T. Orton is quite influential in the area of reading, and will be discussed in the next section, 'The remediation stage'.

This section emphasizes the important contributions made by physicians to the ultimate development of the LD label, and it will conclude with a discussion on the neuropsychiatrist Alfred A. Strauss (1897–1957) — and his associates — who is probably the most significant of all.

The important work of Goldstein in Germany has already been mentioned; and while still in Germany, Strauss served in 1924 as Goldstein's assistant in the Neurological Institute at the University of Frankfurt. Later, Strauss fled Hitler's Germany, and out of necessity, took a circuitous European path before arriving in the United States in 1937. His first European stop in 1933 was Spain, where:

> while serving as a guest professor at the University of Barcelona, he cofounded for the Catalonian government Spain's first govern-mental and private child guidance centers. The latter was a joint effort with Mira y Lopez, head of the Department of Psychiatry at the University. (Cruickshank and Hallahan, 1973, p. 322)

During the Spanish Civil War, anarchists in 1936 seized the Child Guidance Clinic where Strauss worked. He again fled for political reasons, this time to Switzerland, where he had contacts with Jean Piaget, the noted child psychologist. He moved to England in 1937 where he very briefly associated with Lionel S. Penrose on research.

In 1937, Robert H. Haskell, MD, Superintendent of the Wayne

County Training School in Northville, Michigan (which served Detroit), invited Strauss 'to take the position of research psychiatrist in the Training School's research department, which was then directed by . . . Hegge' (Cruickshank and Hallahan, 1973, p. 322).

> Dr. Thorleif G. Hegge, a recent emigrant from Norway, who had a Ph.D. in psychology from Goetingen, Germany, . . . had spent a year in the research department of the Vineland Training School. Dr. Haskell, knowing of . . . Vineland . . . in New Jersey which had become famous through the research contributions of Dr. Henry Goddard and Dr. Edgar Doll, wanted the Wayne County Training School to become famous through research . . . promoting the academic abilities of mentally retarded children and particularly of mentally retarded children who had not learned to read. (Kirk, 1976, p. 246)

The Wayne County Training School, which is no longer in existence, was 'then the world's greatest residential center for educable mentally retarded boys and girls' (Cruickshank, 1976, p. 102). Strauss accepted and arrived in January of 1937. Strauss served as the Training School's Director of Child Care from 1943 until 1946 when ill health forced him to resign.

> In the final years before his death in Chicago on October 27, 1957, he contributed significantly as special lecturer at Wayne State University and Milwaukee State Teachers College, as well as founder of the Cove Schools in Racine, Wisconsin, and cofounder of the Cove Schools in Evanston, Illinois. (Cruickshank and Hallahan, 1973, p. 322)

Strauss followed up his Training School work at the Cove Schools for Brain-injured Children.

Strauss is of utmost importance for two reasons. First and foremost is for his work with brain damaged children and ultimately their education. Though he was fortuitously influenced through personal contact by many of the greatest neurologists and child psychologists whose ideas he absorbed, he was an original thinker. It is also one of the ironies of history that some of these contacts were the result of his flight from political persecution. Secondly, his influence was profound on special educators, during his lifetime and even today.

Heinz Werner (Ph.D., 1890–1964) — a German emigre to America, in 1933 by way of Holland — became Strauss' major research collaborator at the Wayne County School in late 1937. Werner was already a developmental psychologist of great reknown when he arrived in America. Werner, 'accepting an invitation from Walter Pillsbury to come to the

University of Michigan' (Witkin, 1965, p. 310), stayed there for three years continuing his investigations. He was a visiting professor at Harvard for the 1936–37 academic year. When he returned to Michigan to work at the Training School, he was given the position of senior research psychologist. Werner left for Brooklyn College to teach in 1943, but still carried on research in perception and language. In 1947, Werner was appointed at Clark University professor to the Department of Psychology and Education where he remained, in various capacities, until the end (Witkin, 1965).

At the Training School, Strauss was known as the 'idea man', and Werner the 'laboratory scientist' (Cruickshank, 1976, p. 102).

> Strauss had published a paper in 1933, based on the work he had done while still in Germany, in which he discussed the causes of profound mental deficiency. In it he suggested that brain damage was one important cause of retardation, and he and Werner pursued this idea in their work in Michigan. (Ross, 1977, p. 20)

In addition to the important paper discussed above (Strauss, 1933 a),Strauss had one other article published that year, and this other piece (Strauss, 1933 b) was his first whose major emphasis was pedagogy. Examination of the focus of these two articles, which represent much of his last work in Germany, reveals the direction his interests were taking. (Only one other publication, in 1935, would initially appear in German). Therefore, the Wayne County Training School can be considered fertile ground for the elaborate cultivation of Strauss' important new ideas, and the Cove Schools for Brain-injured Children provided the means for their sophisticated harvesting.

Probably the most significant early notion, when looking for the genesis of learning disabilities (LD), can be traced back to that of 'exogenous factors' as causative to 'mental deficiency' in children as delineated by Strauss (1938). This idea led to the establishment of two distinct categories of retardation: retardation as a result of external brain insult or the 'exogenous type', and that without 'brain damage' (familial retardation) or the 'endogenous type' (Martinson and Strauss, 1940). Strauss, together with Werner, the eminent experimentalist, gave a demonstration with slides of their research at the 1940 Annual Meeting of the American Psychological Association. They wrote about their work as follows:

> Goldstein and Gelb have described a disturbance in the differen-tiation of figure and background in brain-injured adult patients. We have attempted, in various experimental situations, to demonstrate the presence of this disturbance in brain-injured children. Two

groups of mentally retarded children were used. The members of the one group showed symptoms of brain lesion, but these were not present in children of the second group. We analyzed their performances on several new visuo-motor and tactile-motor tests and their reactions to patterns presented tachistoscopically. One of the tests consists of copying patterns made up of marbles placed in the holes of a cardboard background. Both the marbles and the holes have a definite configuration. The child must construct the patterns in spite of the influence which the background (hole-) configuration exerts. A tactual-motor test was constructed on similar principles. The pictures used in the tachistoscopic test were drawings of objects embedded in a clearly structured homogeneous background. The child was asked to tell what he saw. The results of the various tests demonstrate that, for the brain-injured child, the characteristics of the background have strong stimulus value, whereas they exert little influence on the reactions of the children having no brain lesion. (Werner and Strauss, 1940, p. 440).

As an aside, some notable professionals who were at the Wayne County Training School, not all of them during Werner and Strauss' tenure, were as follows. Sidney W. Bijou, an experimental behavioral psychologist; Boyd R. McCandless, a child developmental psychologist; Newell Kephart, the author; Bluma B. Weiner, a special educator; Samuel A. Kirk, who was at the Wayne County School from 1931 to 1935 — from the time he received his master's degree until his Ph.D. was conferred from the University of Michigan — where he taught mentally retarded children, did research, and supervised other U. of MI graduate students; and William M. Cruickshank, who did graduate work there with Strauss and Werner after Kirk left (W.M. Cruickshank, personal communication, March 15, 1984; Cruickshank and Hallahan, 1973; Kirk, 1976). Cruickshank would later become one of the most prominent of all special educators.

The quintessential piece of literature representing the work of Werner and Strauss appeared shortly after the Cove Schools were founded, and was actually coauthored by Strauss and Lehtinen (1947); the latter a most important Cove Schools associate. Regarding Strauss, Cruickshank and Hallahan (1973) wrote:

Fully expanded delineations of his techniques for perceptual-motor training and his concept of a structured program within a stimuli reduced environment ... appeared in the classic volumes coauthored with Laura Lehtinen and Newell Kephart (Strauss and Lehtinen, 1947; Strauss and Kephart, 1955). (p. 324)

The Remediation Stage

The remediation stage, circa 1920 to 1962, is chronologically virtually the same as Wiederholt's 'transition phase, circa 1921–1960', and although he did a masterful job with the material he used, Wiederholt's is thought here to be incomplete. He failed to include both the influence of the child study movement in the earlier part and the slow learner period at the end, both of which, though not previously recognized, helped the LD concept come into existence. Out of child study came sanctioned and 'scientific' individual differences which allowed for development of student classification, while the slow learner was the real progenitor of the LD child in search of a more suitable educational label. Wiederholt did, however, properly emphasize the transition. Myers and Hammill (1982) also saw the influence of remediation in schools during this transitory, historical stage.

> During the transition phase . . . a concerted effort was made to translate the theoretical postulates derived in the previous stage into remedial practice. The focus of inquiry shifted from adults to children, and the ideas that had been developed from the study of adults were transferred in total to the study of children with developmental disorders. (p. 23)

Learning disabilities (LD) definitions are by design so broad, they subsume all the academic skills such as reading, spelling, writing, and arithmetic, but also include, and were really derived from, speech and language disorders. A more severe learning disability could therefore logically affect more than a single specific area, and would be a more pervasive problem in terms of educating an individual. However, since reading is such an important aspect in the curriculum of modern literate societies, it has naturally received the most attention within the LD field and contemporary education as a whole.

In the United States, remedial reading as a concept really first evolved in the 1920s (Smith, 1961). The present author conjectures that a greater need for remediation of reading, over other subjects, arose for four major reasons: (a) Population was rapidly growing due to great waves of immigration, primarily European; and industrialization, which made the one room schoolhouse less common, placed greater emphasis on various grade levels. (The importance, origin, and emphasis on grade levels to special education were pointed out in Chapter 2 in conjunction with William Torrey Harris). (b) The practice of studying individual differences among children in schools was accepted. (c) There was a shift in emphasis on the method of teaching reading, probably related to reason one, from orally to silently. 'Around 1900, there was a heavy emphasis on mechanics of word recognition and fluency in oral reading. The 1920's saw the emphasis switch to teaching attitudes and skills concerned with clear and rapid comprehension in silent reading' (Kaluger and Kolson, 1969, p. 3). And (d), just as more sophisticated schooling arrangements helped create the mildly retarded student, so too did they produce the student who required remedial reading by the 1920s.

In the earlier part of the remediation stage physicians still played a major role, and of special importance is the American neurologist Samuel Torrey Orton who influenced virtually all the major remedial reading people, including today's.

> Hinshelwood and Orton had attempted to locate the causative factors of disabilities in reading, writing, spelling, and arithmetic and had suggested some general remedial principles . . . . Fernald, Monroe, Kirk, Gillingham, and Spalding extended the work of Orton by developing specific programs for the remediation of these deficits. (Wiederholt, 1974, p. 132)

The first really systematic remedial approach was the kinesthetic method of teaching, including word tracing, by Grace Fernald and Helen Keller (1921).

> Working with children of normal mentality who had failed to learn to read after 3 or more years in the public schools and who failed to make progress after individualized instruction by recognized methods, they designed the visual-auditory-kinesthetic-tactile (VAKT) approach. (Wiederholt, 1974, p. 132)

Fernald's (1943) more contemporary work, according to Wiederholt (1974), is widely used in LD programs today. Orton (1925) was at first quite interested in the word blindness concept when he worked with Marion Monroe (1928), his research associate, in the Mobile Mental Hygiene Clinic at the Iowa State Psychopathic Hospital. Later, Monroe (1932) leaned more toward auditory discrimination and employed repetition and drill while developing a 'synthetic phonetic approach'. Orton's (1937) more contemporary work — which became very well known and influential — stressed that those students who have trouble in reading, writing and speech have faulty development of the necessary one-sided dominance in brain control resulting in a condition he called 'strephosymbolia' that literally translates as twisted symbols. Strephosymbolia, according to Orton, 'was remediated by the teaching of the phonetic equivalents of printed letters and by the process of blending sequences rather than by the then popular whole-word or sight-word method' (Wiederholt, 1974, p. 119).

All the major remedial reading systems from the mid-1930s and those to follow (Gillingham and Stillman, 1936; Hegge, Kirk and Kirk, 1936; Spalding and Spalding, 1962) emphasized phonics training. That is, the application of phonetics (or the science of the sounds of language) to reading (Kaluger and Kolson, 1969). Reading disability today is still viewed as a language disorder (Siegel and Ryan, 1984). Helmer Myklebust (1955) and Mildred A. McGinnis along with her colleagues (1956), who had backgrounds in deaf education, also made pioneering contributions to remedial treatment procedures for aphasic children.

Inspired by the work of Strauss and Werner (1941) on 'brain-injured' mentally retarded children plus the landmark book by Strauss in collaboration with Laura E. Lehtinen (Strauss and Lehtinen, 1947), a number of remedial programs for perceptual-motor impaired and hyperactive-distractible youngsters were designed in the last few years of the remediation period. Some mention is necessary of Lehtinen who 'developed not so much a specific method as a teaching procedure based on Strauss' research and on his theory of cortical damage. The fact that her pioneering efforts have not been outmoded attests to their validity' (Myers and Hammill, 1969, p. 135).

> Lehtinen offered the following modifications in the classroom environment: (*a*) The classroom should be arranged with simplicity to protect the child from distraction. (*b*) Grouping should remain small with explicit and orderly procedures. (*c*) Routine should be established, so that the child can predict the day's events. (*d*) Desks should face the wall, so that the presence of other children does not serve as a distraction. (Wiederholt, 1974, p. 137)

Newell Kephart, who worked with Strauss (Strauss and Kephart, 1955), and Carl H. Delacato (1959) stressed (body) motor development training to increase school skills. Delacato's primary professional interest was reading, and to some extent speech, to which he tied his theory of mixed laterality as demonstrative of improper central nervous system development. Delacato, simply put, therefore advocated practice in physical tasks of earlier sensorimotor development to improve reading and this notion has evoked much criticism. The optometrist Gerald N. Getman (1962) and Raymond H. Barsch (1963, 1966, 1967) designed activities for training visual-motor skills while William Cruickshank and associates (e.g., Cruickshank, Bentzen, Ratzeburg and Tannhauser, 1961) 'combined Strauss's orientation with Lehtinen's instructional techniques and applied them to teaching the nonretarded, perceptually impaired, hyperactive child' (Myers and Hammill, 1982, p. 24). Cruickshank became an early leader in the education of cerebral palsied (CP) children, and he gave much credit for this to Jane Dolphin-Courtney (1950), his first doctoral candidate-student. 'If the findings of Dolphin were correct and if the perceptual disabilities noted in cerebral-palsied children were similar to the exogenous mentally retarded subjects, could other groups of neurologically handicapped children be likewise penalized?' (Cruickshank, 1976, p. 104). It seemed logical that children of average intelligence with neurological problems would have the same symptoms as Strauss and Werner's exogenous mentally retarded ones; and it also made sense to try perceptual-motor skill training with such children, especially CP youngsters who are physically handicapped.

In order to remediate a learning deficit most successfully, the exact nature of the problem should be known as precisely as possible. Therefore, a number of tests of varying sophistication were developed during the later remediation period. Some of the more famous follow. Jon Eisenson (1954) developed the quite thorough *Examining for aphasia* instrument, and he 'believed that children with aphasic disturbances had difficulty in symbolic abilities' and 'experienced intellectual changes' (Wiederholt, 1974, p. 131). Joseph Wepman (1958) is most well known for the *Auditory discrimination test* which assesses recognition of the differences between English language phonemes which he believed to be related to speech and reading. Samuel A. Kirk and James J. McCarthy (1961) developed 'The Illinois test of psycho-linguistic abilities' (ITPA). The ITPA's authors were very much influenced by the ideas of Charles Osgood (1953), but also by Wepman's (1960) — who Wiederholt (1974) referred to as diagram makers, or in more modern terms, model builders — and perhaps also by Dorothy J. Sievers (1955, 1956). Sievers, one of Kirk's doctoral students at the University of Illinois, devoted her dissertation to a test of preschooler psycholinguistic development. The ITPA has a basal age of $2\frac{1}{3}$ years and a ceiling of $10\frac{1}{4}$ years. In addition to tests of language, tests for visual-memory, visual-perception, and visual-motor functioning were developed to determine the extent of non-language perceptual deficits, if any, which were thought to adversely affect the acquisition of academic skills. The 'Developmental test of visual-perception' (Frostig, Lefever and Whittlesey, 1961), Lauretta Bender's (1938) 'Visual motor gestalt test' and Arthur L. Benton's (1945) 'Visual retention test' are some of the earlier ones and most well known. They are all still used, while Elizabeth Munsterberg Koppitz's (1963) adaptation of Bender's test for children enjoys enormous popularity with school psychologists today.

The Slow Learner Period

Work about the slow learner can be found as early as the mid-1930s (Ingram, 1935, 1953, 1960). However, it is within the late 1950s and 1960s that the slow learner received overwhelming attention (Benyon, 1968; Cleugh, 1957; G.O. Johnson, 1963; Karlin and Berger, 1969; Kephart, 1960; Younie, 1967); and this was an era that spanned a time from slightly before the actual LD conception to the real beginnings of its institutionalization. This was the time when the post-World War II baby-boom had burst upon the scene. All of these children had to be educated. The slow learner concept filled a needed slot in the intellectual-achievement hierarchy of schooling, and its result was the fulfillment of a temporary vacuum in the schooling schemata of American education. A good characterization of the slow learner is 'the child who is not able to keep up with the normal progress of the class, but who is too bright to place in an EMR class' (Gaddis, 1971, p. 5).

The slow learner concept still had momentum into the 1970s (Cawley, Goodstein and Burrow, 1972; Ellis, 1973; Gaddis, 1971; Haigh, 1977; Kephart, 1960, 1971; Shelton, 1971) even though LD classes were becoming entrenched within American public schools. The slow learner material is still taught today to graduate special education students and prospective LD specialists, often with Kephart's (1960–1971) book, much of which is devoted to perceptual training. Remember, Strauss and Kephart (1955) had collaborated earlier. Ross (1977) discusses Kephart (1960–1971): 'When the first edition of this book appeared in 1960, it was unique in its concrete recommendations of how the teacher might deal with the "slow learner" ' (p. 193).

As was pointed out in Chapter 2, mandated special classes for the educationally retarded were first required by law in 1911, beginning in New Jersey. All the other states eventually followed suit due to mandatory student attendance laws which were universal by 1918. In the 1920s, the remediation stage was born. It is the contention here that the next significant intellectual movement in American education was that of the 'slow learner period' which began in the 1930s. The combination of the accepted mind-set of labeling students (attributed to G. Stanley Hall and his students), work about brain damaged children (by Strauss and his disciples), and the very pregnant notion of the slow learner, gave birth to the learning disabilities label. These three areas — described immediately above — helped set the stage for even more advanced research in learning problems and made for a close relationship between medicine and education.

Initial Establishment of the LD Label as a Clinical Entity

Reflecting on the slow learner, we find a type of child who needs help in school but is really in educational limbo. The problem is recognized, but there is no special place for such a student, who is in the regular classroom, except for occasional time spent in the remedial teachers' cubbyholes.

By the mid-1950s to early 1960s, Strauss' work was becoming fairly widely disseminated. Some of the more sophisticated parents, whose children had problems in school, were aware of Strauss' ideas, and started taking action; parent groups were actually the driving force for the ultimate acceptance of the LD label as a clinical entity.

> Parents who were convinced that Strauss' views perceptively described their children welcomed the theories of diagnosis and treatment presented by Strauss. However, these parents soon discovered that educators, physicians, and psychologists were generally unaware of the concepts that Strauss had evolved and of the educational treatment that he had suggested. These parents, believing that public schools should provide the special education required for their children, organized parent groups for the purpose of convincing schools that these exceptional children were educable and that it was the obligation of the schools to provide appropriate education. As has been typical within the history of special education, the pressure and impetus came from parent groups rather than from educators. (Lerner, 1971, pp. 21–22)

The attitude taken by the parents described above is not surprising in light of the following statement from Strauss and Kephart (1955). 'We must therefore expand our concept of brain injury to include children with "normal" I.Q.'s' (p. 2). It must be remembered that Strauss and Werner's earlier work had dealt with the retarded. Also from Strauss and Kephart (1955) is the passage below.

> . . . new ideas and theories in neurology and psychiatry, apparently will permit us to see a definite clinical syndrome. That such endeavor may lead not only to theoretical understanding of brain injury in children but may also lead to a more effective treatment of so-called 'normal' brain-injured children — they may be diagnosed as 'cerebral palsy' or as 'behavior problem' — is not a minor consideration, but is a goal toward which we are intensely devoted as physicians and educators. (p. ix)

It is easily seen how the parents of non-retarded, physically intact children with learning problems could be greatly aroused by the above statements. It is important to note that the mention of 'behavior problem' above is primarily in reference to hyperactivity thought to be the result of brain damage; and that the hyperactive child of normal IQ, with or without a learning problem but usually with one, was later to be referred to as having the 'Strauss syndrome' which was first suggested by Godfrey D. Stevens and Jack W. Birch (1957). Stevens and Birch describe their newly named syndrome.

> In detail, the child with central nervous system impairment may show any or most of the following observable characteristics:
> 1. Erratic and inappropriate behavior on mild provocation.
> 2. Increased motor activity disproportionate to the stimulus.
> 3. Poor organization of behavior.
> 4. Distractibility of more than ordinary degree under ordinary conditions.
> 5. Persistent faulty perceptions.
> 6. Persistent hyperactivity.
> 7. Awkwardness and consistently poor motor performance. (p. 348)

By the early 1960s, much terminology, which implied the cause of children's learning problems, was promulgated. Some terms, suggested by the more influential special educators are 'brain-injured child' by Cruickshank, 'perceptually handicapped child' by Kephart (Cruickshank, personal communication, March 8 1984), 'learning disabilities' by Kirk (1962) and 'minimal brain dysfunction' (MBD) by Sam D. Clements and J.E. Peters (1962).

From 1959 to 1960 many parent groups were formed to promote Strauss' ideas in order to better serve children with learning difficulties (Lerner, 1971). Two of the most influential groups were the New York Association for Brain-Injured Children (a state-wide group) and in Evanston, Illinois was the Fund for Perceptually Handicapped Children, both formed in 1957. In 1960 the California Association for Neurologically Handicapped Children was founded.

Chicago in April of 1963 was the site of 'The Conference on Exploration into Problems of the Perceptually Handicapped Child', sponsored by the group headquartered in Evanston, IL. Kirk was one of a number of interested professionals invited to speak at this conference (see Kirk, 1963, for the content of his talk there which is the lead article in the conference *Proceedings*); and before his address, several of the sponsoring group approached him 'with the admonition that they needed help in the selection of a name for their proposed national organization' (Kirk, 1976, p. 255). The evening Kirk gave his speech at the 1963 Conference, 'the convention voted to organize itself as The Association for Children with Learning Disabilities (ACLD)' (Wiederholt, 1974, p. 142).

In 1964, the Council of Exceptional Children (CEC) — a well established national association that promotes quality education for all types of disabled children — held their annual conference in Chicago. A significant meeting of fifteen or so people occurred, which Dr. Cruickshank attended, at the Morrison Hotel during the course of this conference (Cruickshank, personal communication, March 15, 1984).

> At the invitation of Dr. Kirk, some . . . professional people met in a hotel room . . . to see if we could or would utilize the term 'learning disabilities', which had been put forth more or less accidently by parents a year earlier. There was an easily reached agreement because we generally all had come from the same orientation, even to the point where six . . . had worked together in the same institution. . . . It was a 25-year professional honeymoon of the most satisfying order. Today this is not so. (Cruickshank, 1983, p. 191)

(That institution in common, above, was the Wayne County Training School). Two significant things happened after this meeting. First, CEC formed a Division for Children with Learning Disabilities (DCLD). (The DCLD seceded from CEC a few years ago and is now the CLD. The CLD's orientation is along the lines of what this writer calls the 'newer practice model', which is discussed in a later subchapter. The CEC — after DCLD withdrew — formed the DLD which has a more traditional outlook on LD). Second, and more importantly, LD was accepted for its generality, because it is a term less noxious than the others, and it is more educationally relevant; but its generality automatically subsumes the other terms, e.g., MBD.

One final note to this subchapter is necessary. Even though LD is used in schools, it is generally understood or explained as signifying minor brain damage even today. The Strauss syndrome or MBD are today known as the 'attention deficit disorder' with or without hyperactivity, according to the *Diagnostic and statistical manual of mental disorders, third edition* (DSM-III) (American Psychiatric Association, 1980). LD is not a DSM-III category; but listed under 'developmental disorders' are reading, arithmetic, language, articulation, mixed specific, and atypical disorders.

Institutionalization of LD as an Educational Arrangement

In the previous subchapter the birth of the the LD label as a clinical entity was discussed. In this, it will be shown how this new entity in American education was utilized to place children in separate special education programs. We must begin with the work of Samuel A. Kirk, who more than anyone else, has been instrumental in popularizing the LD concept.

The first book where a formal discussion, albeit brief, and definition of 'learning disabilities' appeared, was one by Kirk (1962).

> A learning disability refers to a *retardation, disorder, or delayed development in one or more of the processes of speech, language, reading, spelling, writing, or arithmetic* resulting from a possible cerebral dysfunction and/or emotional or behavioral disturbance and not from mental retardation, sensory deprivation, or cultural or instructional factors. (Kirk, 1962, p. 263, all italicized in original).

LD was also seen in 1962 for the first time in a journal article: 'Diagnosis and remediation of learning disabilities' (Kirk and Bateman, 1962 — this definition is found in Chapter 1 of this work). The definitions given in both are nearly identical except the Kirk definition includes 'spelling' while the Kirk and Bateman one does not. The latter does, however, discuss spelling in the sentence immediately preceeding the definition and it includes the phrase 'or other school subjects' which actually makes it some-what more educationally inclusive.

Despite his writings of 1962, Kirk (1976) later wrote that:

> Although I did not originate the term 'specific learning disabilities', it has been attributed to me because (1) I used the term in 1962 in my book on exceptional children . . . and (2) I later (1963) suggested the term as the least objectionable to parents' groups organizing ACLD. (p. 257)

This is technically accurate, but the term 'specific learning disability', as far as is known, was used first in print by Kirk (1962, p. 263). The word *specific* is not used in Kirk and Bateman (1962). Two earlier journal titles — 'Specific dyslexia (congenital word-blindness): A clinical and genetic study' (Hallgren, 1950–51) and 'Specific reading disability – Strephosymbolia' (Orton, 1928) — are quite similar to specific learning disability. The Orton reference is cited in the second edition of Kirk's (1962–1972) *Educating exceptional children*, while both Orton and Hallgren are cited in the third edition of this book (Kirk and Gallagher, 1962–1979). Attention to this sort of detail is useful as Kirk's terminology and definitions from his 1962 works form the basis for later legal definitions and subsequent government sponsored programs via legislation. In addition, even though Kirk's early definitions were nearly universally accepted as proposed for the sake of providing special programs for previously unserved students, LD definitions have always been a topic of debate in special education (including LD) journals and many authors of books on LD provide their own variation.

Public Law 88–164 (see Table 2 on federal legislation in Chapter 2), which was signed into law by President Kennedy in October of 1963, provided funds for the training of personnel for work with various types of handicapped children including 'crippled, or other health impaired, who by reason thereof require special education and related services'. Although PL88–164 listed a number of handicapping conditions, LD was not among them. LD–type students were later *considered* to be within the other health impaired group. Kirk — who served as Director of the Division of Exceptional Children and Youth, US Office of Education, from February to June 1964 — wrote:

> Having been appointed as the director of a newly created Division of Handicapped Children in the federal Office of Education, *I interpreted 'other health impaired' to include learning disabilities*, under the assumption that learning disabled children have a central dysfunction which interferes with their development. Four colleges and universities obtained grants in 1964 to train personnel in learning disabilities. A few research grants in learning disabilities or related areas were also awarded. This development of federal subsidy for the preparation of personnel in learning disabilities has continued since that date. (Kirk, 1976, p. 256; emphasis added)
>
> In 1966 a unit on Learning Disorders and Interrelated Areas was added to the Division of Training Programs, Bureau of Education for the Handicapped, United States Office of Education. Funding for children with learning disabilities was, therefore, for the first time distinguished from 'crippled and other health impaired'. (Senf, 1981, p. 94)

With the phrase LD, despite its implied meaning of neurologic disorganization, having gained coinage over the more medical-organic sounding terms, such as minimal brain dysfunction, a closer alliance with education came about. The next logical step, therefore, would be to formulate a more educationally useful definition of LD; and an event took place to do this.

> A milestone in defining learning disabilities within an educational perspective was reached through an Advanced Study Institute held at Northwestern University in 1967. This institute, attended by 15 special educators, forged an educational definition to supercede the existing multi-disciplinary definitions. (Senf, 1981, p. 94)

This Study Institute's 1967 definition is below.

Learning disability refers to one or more significant deficits in essential learning processes requiring special education techniques for remediation. Children with learning disability generally demonstrate a discrepancy between expected and actual achievement in one or more areas, such as spoken, read, or written language, mathematics, and spatial orientation. The learning disability referred to is not primarily the result of sensory, motor, intellectual, or emotional handicap, or lack of opportunity to learn.

Significant deficits are defined in terms of accepted diagnostic procedures in education and psychology.

Essential learning processes are those currently referred to in behavioral science as involving perception, integration, and expression either verbal or nonverbal.

Special education techniques for remediation refers to educational planning based on diagnostic procedures and results. (Kass and Myklebust, 1969, p. 39)

For a field of professional activity to become truly legitimized, not only are associations needed, but so too are journals. The first issue of the *Journal of Learning Disabilities* was introduced in January of 1968 — published by the Professional Press in Chicago — and proclaimed to be 'multi-disciplinary', a 'clinical exchange', and 'international'. The Kirk and Bateman (1962) article, the first about LD, came out in a special education journal with a long history called *Exceptional Children*. (*Learning Disability Quarterly*, sponsored by DCLD, was to publish its inaugural issue as of 'Winter 1978'. A few other lesser LD journals appeared shortly after DCLD's, and numerous articles about LD appeared in other, newer special education journals not solely devoted to any one disability). The *Journal of Learning Disabilities'* first article, by Ray H. Barsch (1968), has a most incisive title as it relates to the LD field: 'Perspectives on learning disabilities: The vectors of a new convergence'. As was demonstrated by the earlier 'Essential precursors' subchapter, Barsch's notion of vectors converging is really on target for introducing the field's own, initial journal.

In the late 1960s and to the latter part of the 1970s — before any major involvement on the part of the US federal government in special education — states that were leaders in special education, generally those with powerful parent groups and/or those with professionals in their state universities acquainted with LD, already had many special educational programs in place including those for LD youngsters. With a growing awareness but much confusion about LD because of conflicting statements given it, particularly over estimates of the LD incidence rate ranging from 2 to 30 per cent of the school population, Congress authorized the National Advisory Committee for the Handicapped, chaired by Kirk, to clarify such issues (Kirk, 1976). 'The Committee estimated that from 1 to 3 percent of school children are likely to have a specific learning disability' (Kirk, 1976, p. 257), and also offered the following definition of LD.

> Children with special learning disabilities exhibit a disorder in one or more of the basic psychological processes involved in understanding or in using spoken or written language. These may be manifested in disorders of listening, thinking, talking, reading, writing, spelling, or arithmetic. They include conditions which have been referred to as perceptual handicaps, brain injury, minimal brain dysfunction, dyslexia, developmental aphasia, etc. They do not include learning problems which are due primarily to visual, hearing, or motor handicaps, to mental retardation, emotional disturbance, or to environmental disadvantage. (National Advisory Committee, 1968, p. 14)

Based on the Committee's report, Congress passed the Learning Disability Act of 1969 (see Table 2). However, 'No appropriation of money was made for these services' (Kirk, 1976, p. 257) at that time.

The situation remained static for almost another decade. That is, LD classes were still optional for the states, but this was to change dramatically. In 1975, Congress passed Public Law 94–142, The Education for All Handicapped Children Act. Under PL94–142, which became effective October 1 1977, all states were required to provide for, and would be reimbursed for, all children formally classified as educationally handicapped — including LD children. Up until very late 1977, the federal government funded research, demonstration projects, and professional training to varying degrees related to the education of LD children, but did not directly fund their education en masse. PL94–142's definition of 'specific learning disability' following is virtually the same as the Committee's (1968) definition of 'special learning disabilities' except for a few slight differences in wording at the beginning.

> 'Specific learning disability' means a disorder in one or more of the basic psychological processes involved in understanding or in using language, spoken or written, which may manifest itself in an imperfect ability to listen, think, speak, read, write, spell, or to do mathematical calculations. The term includes such conditions as perceptual handicaps, brain injury, minimal brain dysfunction, dyslexia, and developmental aphasia. The term does not include children who have learning problems which are primarily the result of visual, hearing, or motor handicaps, of mental retardation, or of environmental, cultural or economic disadvantage. (Education of Handicapped, 1977, p. 42478)

The essence of Kirk's (1962) original LD definition never really changed during the thirteen years it took to become legally institutionalized.

The metamorphosis is now complete. The clinical entity, for which the many vectors took so long to converge, was legitimized by the US Congress. As a result, new formalized 'special' school tracks were mandated.

Contemporary Practice

This subchapter covers salient historical points concerning conventional wisdom within the LD field since its modern inception — circa 1962. In very broad terms, there has been a sequential shift over time in the major areas of emphasis within the contemporary LD field. Yet, thought on the previous major areas of emphasis continues to be influential in actual school practice even after being supplanted by newer ideas. The research-educators, usually at universities, would be in the vanguard of each succeeding new wave, while school practitioners would generally learn of these new advances much later.

First there was the emphasis on brain injury, primarily as a result of the work by Strauss but also Cruickshank. Next there was the shift to perception or perceptual motor function exemplified by Kephart and also Barsch. Then came the stress on language (Bannatyne, 1971; Kirk, McCarthy and Kirk, 1968). The major area of interest in the LD field today is cognitive. This author suggests, that out of the cognitive area, there is now emerging another important major area which is called 'interactionism'. Specifically, the cognitive in relation to interactionism is the newer practice model (discussed in the next subchapter), but it is not at this time a fully recognized major area. Because cognition — as the term is now used in the LD field — is the current major area of LD emphasis, and is giving birth to LD interactionism, its roots will be pointed out here.

The cognitive area stresses the learning process, and can be traced back to B.F. Skinner's (1965) classic lecture named 'The technology of teaching' delivered on November 19 1964. Also of great importance to this area is Siegfried Englemann (1969) who used Skinnerian principles and started with the disadvantaged, not the handicapped. Englemann recommended a task analysis which is:

> an outgrowth of behavioristic psychology and an essential component of behavior modification. This approach demands that educational objectives be operationally stated, that the task be broken down into small sequential components, and that required

appropriate responses be specified for each step in the sequential hierarchy. (Tarver and Hallahan, 1976, p. 48)

Other Skinnerian psychologists did, however, work with special education students using 'applied behavioral analysis' (the ABA model) which involves time on task, associated learning variables, student self-charting, etc. Probably the best large sampling for this type of work from that era is found in a large edited book entitled *An empirical basis for change in education: Selections on behavioral psychology for teachers* (Becker, 1971).

Similar to ABA is 'direct instruction' which involves teaching, in a highly attentive manner, weak academic areas. When direct instruction is used, the type or source of the assumed dysfunction does not matter. This is in sharp contrast with remediating faulty internal psycholinguistic (Kirk, 1966) or weak intra-psychic perceptual (Johnson and Myklebust, 1967) processes which first:

> involves determination of the perceptual channels required in understanding the task and making the required responses, whether the task is essentially unisensory or crossmodal, . . . verbal or non-verbal. . . . Johnson and Myklebust's (1967) task analysis approach seems to lend itself to process-oriented remediation, while the approach of Engelmann (1969) seems to be more appropriate for tool-oriented remediation. (Tarver and Hallahan, 1976, p. 48)

Some fine examples of direct instruction are Becker and Carnine (1982), Carnine (1979), Englemann (1969), and Englemann and Carnine (1969). Direct instruction also emphasizes good, rigorous teaching methods which require a great deal of preparation, and has evoked thought about 'precision teaching'.

The Newer Practice Model

The 'newer practice model' of LD herein refers to methods, techniques, and strategies — rather than for work about LD as a particular clinical entity — to facilitate the learning and adjustment of students who have difficulty with the conventional school program. Further, there is here absolutely no underlying assumption that there is within the student any faulty intrapsychic process disorder. This is not to deny, however, that there may in fact be an underlying individual neurological or emotional disorder — as these of course do exist — which will prevent learning or social adjustment even under the most humane and favorable conditions. In addition, these techniques, methods, and strategies to augment conventional schooling can and should be used in both regular and special education programs at all intellectual levels. Finally, although methods developed in the earlier history of special education for obvious moderately to severely handicapped students (such as the blind, deaf, physically handicapped, those with definite hard signs of neurological impairment, retarded, autistic, or seriously emotionally disturbed) can and should in some cases be used with the so-called mildly handicapped or regular education students, much of the recent work in special education has specifically focused on the mild group.

It can be said that the newer practice model has its formal beginnings with the work of the five contemporary federally funded LD research institutes (see in Table 2 details about their establishment and purpose under PL91–230 of 1970), and also in what appears to be the beginning of a major shift in attitude about LD as a clinical label. Earlier, there were 97 Child Service Demonstration Centers (CSDCs) with at least one in every state and Puerto Rico, to serve the learning disabled, funded through grants under PL91–230 (see Table 2 and Mann *et al.*, 1984). However, in 1977, 'the Bureau of Education for the Handicapped (now Special Education Programs) sent out a request for proposals to fund five learning disabilities research institutes' (Kneedler and Hallahan, 1983, p. viii). The purpose of the five institutes was to move beyond the work of the CSDCs which variously operated from about 1971 to 1980. Although the Centers had as their primary mission the provision of 'effective educational services and training, . . . many conceptual and educational concerns surfaced' (Deshler, 1978, p. 68). Hence, the perceived need for the institutes which began operations in 1977 or 1978 and started to wind down in 1982 or 1983.

The institutes as a whole came away with two findings of paramount importance. The first was that there were 'independently identified several similar directions for effective intervention with the LD child and adolescent' (Kneedler and Hallahan, 1983, p. ix). These similar directions came from the four of five LD research institutes that actively sought to develop worthwhile techniques to counteract poor school adjustment and learning difficulties — they are: the University of Illinois at Chicago Circle, the University of Virginia, the University of Kansas, and Teachers College of Columbia University. At Teachers College the researchers concentrated on academic strategies and were guided by the hypothesis that the disabled learner has difficulty cognitively processing information.

> In fact, it can be postulated that the academic failure experienced by learning disabled children results from an interaction between the way they process information and the information-processing demands of the instructional methods in use in their classrooms.
>
> If this is the case, there are two options for remedial instruc-tion. Under one option, the variables in instructional methods can be manipulated to make instruction more effective and efficient.

The second option focuses directly on the student rather than the method of instruction. Under this option, the learning disabled child is taught to use effective and efficient strategies for processing the information he or she is expected to master. (Connor, 1983, pp. 23–24)

In the Chicago institute, the primary focus was on treatment techniques for social competence with quite an academic ring. 'Studies included investigations of LD children's communicative competence (e.g., adapting one's style to listeners, conversational skills), . . . causal attributions of success and failure' (Bryan, Pearl, Donahue, Bryan and Pflaum, 1983, p. 1), and metacognitive reading deficits for which the concern is with the relations between and among words in sentences. The LD institutes at Kansas and Virginia — which dealt almost exclusively with adolescents and elementary school students, respectively — were concerned with 'active student involvement in the learning process and. . . . both . . . borrowed heavily from the work of the Chicago researchers' (Kneedler and Hallahan, 1983, p. viii). The second major finding was based on the work of the fifth institute located at the University of Minnesota which focused on identification of the LD student. The Institute for Research on Learning Disabilities, University of MN, found there is virtually no difference between the underachieving pupil and the so-called mildly handicapped LD. student as determined through current procedures usually used by local school districts across America for purposes of formal classification.

In essence then, it is suggested that the newer practice model, in general, stresses three basic notions. (a) Firstly, sophisticated remedial techniques, which often are actually of a metacognitive nature, are efficacious. That is, metacognitive processes operate on other processes (thoughts about behavioral strategies), while cognitive processes operate on data, e.g., $2 + 2 = 4$ (Robert J. Sternberg, personal communication, September 12, 1984). (b) There is the recognition that what has greatly come under the umbrella of special education in recent years would more appropriately be considered within the realm of remedial education. Examine, for example, the titles of two recent publications, one a book and the other a professional journal. They are *Critical issues in special and remedial education* (Ysseldyke and Algozzine, 1982) and *Remedial and Special Education* whose January/February 1984 issue was its first after absorbing three other contemporary and now defunct special education tomes. (It was formerly *Exceptional Education Quarterly* and integrated *Topics in Learning & Learning Disabilities* as well as the *Journal for Special Educators*.) (c) The third notion about the newer practice model is that a more sensible, interactionistic approach is applied when dealing with the so-called mild LD or underachieving student.

Examples are below. The Chicago LD institute used an 'interactionist pers-pective' so that 'attentions were directed more toward changing teacher behavior and classroom structures than toward changing curricula, although there were some efforts in this direction as well' (Bryan *et al.*, 1983, p. 2). Schumaker and Deshler (1983), from the Kansas LD institute, directly base their 'learning strategies approach' on 'Lewin's (1935) model that views behavior as a function of the interaction between the characteristics of learner variables and environmental variables' (p. 3). The Columbia University institute also stressed poor interaction as causative to learning disablement. The last example of this approach is from Gerald M. Senf (at this writing, editor-in-chief of the *Journal of Learning Disabilities*), who calls for a 'child-school interaction model' because 'The critical issue is not the labeling of some disorder, but the localization of the problem(s) through an analysis of the child-school interaction so that a more optimizing interaction can be found' (Senf, 1981, p. 121).

The problem with the earlier process orientation of LD was that it dealt only with internal traits, obvious or inferred; obvious meaning severe brain injury and inferred for the mild process disorder. The more recent strict cognitive LD orientation relies too heavily on the behavioral approach. The contrast of these two orientations is reminiscent, to some degree, of the earlier debate in psychology circles over whether heredity or environment is more important to the individual's development. Moreover, in as much as the direction of the modern LD field has been set by psy-chologists (Blatt, 1982; Tomlinson, 1982), it is unsurprising that the LD field could shift toward interactionism because psychology seems also to be going in this direction (Sigmon, 1984a, 1984b). The newer practice model, which stresses the individual's interaction with the social milieu, is fortunately the direction in which the vanguard of the LD field seems to be moving.

Summary

The field of learning disabilities was characterized as 'vectors of a new con-vergence' (Barsch, 1968) in the first issue of the *Journal of Learning Disabilities*. This certainly is true. LD's varied origins were derived from disorders of language (written and/or spoken), perceptual processes, and perceptual motor functioning. The study of such disorders was first done by general physicians, ophthalmologists, but mostly by neurologists, and later by educators interested in remediation. There is general agreement about this.

From the contemporary radical perspective, we can also see the cultural influences that shaped the direction LD took, in addition to the narrow functional historical account. For instance, psychologist Hall and his students, at the beginning of the twentieth century, provided the legitima-tion for studying individual differences among school children. (Further, the result of child study is not always to the advantage of individual students at school — especially for the poor and foreign born, primarily in relation to IQ tests.) Cultural acceptance of individual differences led to the establish-ment of special classes, most of which were for the so-called mildly retarded.

With categorization and segregation of many mildly retarded students having become accepted practice through inferential test data, other types would also be discovered and be so treated. The idea of the brain damaged student of average intelligence merged with the notion of the slow learning child to become LD. This filled a void in American education to help deal with other academic non-conforming students. LD then, instead of becom-ing the basis for sophisticated remediation which was a possibility, became institutionalized and produced new special segregated tracks. Moreover, the rationale for placement of LD children in special education is that there is within the child some intrapsychic disorder. This kind of rationale leads us to controversy.

Chapter 4

The LD Controversy:
A Radical Socioeducational Analysis

The concept of learning disabilities is mysterious and complex. . . .
you must accept one fundamental fact: The field has not yet been reliably
charted. The best any surveyor can do is to stake out some potentially
revealing domains.
Sylvia Farnham-Diggory (1978, p. 1)

Introduction

At this junction it is asked: What are the social and historical roots of the
LD controversy and how would a radical socioeducational analysis (RSA)
explain it? In an effort to answer this question, three major areas of inquiry
are pursued. The first area covered is basically concerned with general
problems of labeling and testing. This is followed by a subchapter dealing
mainly with present LD problems. Finally, the third major subchapter
explores the novel 'reproduction-resistance dialectic' notion, social class
conflict, and the possibilities of interactionism applied to current LD
problems.

Previous Special Education Labeling Controversies and
Newer Developments

The EMR Label

The passage of federal legislation in the mid-1970s (PL94-142) promised that
all children in need of special education would receive it; and that those not
in need of it, or not too much of it, would not be unnecessarily segregated
through due process procedures. This latter issue was especially germane to
the poor and ethnic minorities who were dramatically over-represented in
classes for the mild or educable mentally retarded (EMR). Concurrent to

passage and implementation of PL94-142 was litigation (the most famous of which is the case of Larry P. v. Wilson Riles, 1979, in California) about such over-representation whose end result was a court mandated de-emphasis on the over-reliance of IQ tests for placement of students in EMR classes. The use of IQ tests unilaterally as the basis for special class placement decisions was deemed by the courts to be illegal because of IQ tests' inherent built-in biases against ethnic minorities, many of whom are poor. Other states that were not subjected to such litigation voluntarily promulgated guidelines similar to the courts' admonitions (e.g., New Jersey Department of Education, 1980). With these court decisions and new guidelines, the EMR population, most all of which was segregated within self-contained special classes, would have to decline.

Recent Developments In Cognitive Testing

It has been generally accepted by now that no intelligence test — and probably no test of any kind, although there might be less consensus on this — can ever really be 'culture-free'. In a previous study, Sigmon (1983b) examined a nonverbal, non-motoric spatial abstract reasoning test (Raven's Colored Progressive Matrices Scale) developed in Scotland for schoolchildren which could be considered a 'culture-reduced' measure as it is not verbal information dependent. Yet, even with Raven's Matrices, the more affluent were found to consistently outperform their less advantaged age and/or grade peers in every American study on it. Nevertheless, Sigmon (1983b) developed 'hypothetical national mean raw scores' for the Matrices — as this American data were previously unavailable — in an effort to provide an alternative or at least a supplement to currently widely used culturally biased IQ tests in the USA such as the Stanford-Binet Intelligence Scale, Form L-M, and the Wechsler Intelligence Scale for Children - Revised (WISC-R). Additionally, to further distance cognitive testing from IQs, Sigmon (1984c) devised a procedure whereby Raven's Colored Matrices Scale could denote, fairly precisely, where a child's level of thinking ability is located along the four stage Piagetian thought development continuum. However, even with this utilization of Piaget's stages of development as a theoretical basis for cognitive assessment, the problem of class bias is still encountered. The research of Buck-Morss (1975) indicated the life span time required for higher socioeconomic status (SES) youngsters to achieve Piaget's abstract formal reasoning, the highest stage, is less than that for low SES children; and therefore, drew the conclusion that Piaget's theory of general childhood thought development is social class bound.

There have recently been developed unidimensional tests that are based upon 'latent-trait models which provide sample-free estimates of ability with equal-interval measurement characteristics' (Elliott, 1983, p. 60) such as the British Abilities Scale (BAS). Colin Elliott's BAS relies upon some very straightforward valid notions of test construction and statistical technique. Elliott (1983) claims that conventional tests such as the WISC-R are non-unidimensional and are not really 'measurements' at all in the normally used scientific sense, as they are:

> essentially . . . concerned with *nominal* categorization into groups or with *ordinal* characteristics, i.e. with placing individuals in a group in a rank order. For a test to provide measurements, on the other hand, the numerical scale values should at least have sample-free equal-interval scale characteristics. (pp. 59–60) Non-unidimensional tests can only provide relatively crude estimates of developmental level and should be considered as assessment devices and not as measuring instruments. (p. 88)

By providing sample-free estimates of development, a person's ability is located upon the BAS as, by analogy, a particular length would be on a yardstick. In other words, 'estimates are expressed in units which do not relate to any particular sample or group of individuals within the population' (Elliott, 1983, p. 60). The units are determined via a 'latent trait' or 'Rasch model' using the non-directly observable statistical factor analysis method. The BAS is concerned with the probability of a particular person passing a specific test item based only on two variables — the ability of the person and the difficulty of the item.

The BAS is by far the most sophisticated psychometric device ever devised to test intelligence (and achievement) while completely side-stepping the issue of social class bias. The ostensive neutrality of Elliott's friendly IQ testing with the implication that it can be used for no harmful purpose whatsoever is reminiscent of the illogical old saw used by anti-guncontrol groups: 'People kill, guns don't'. We must be aware of the old inherent problems of tests in new forms.

Other Special Education Labeling Problems

Concomitantly, there has also been concern over the years that too many of the poor and ethnic minorities — who are often viewed as deviant, during the course of their struggle to subsist, by the dominant host culture — would be placed in special classes or schools for the emotionally disturbed or socially maladjusted. (The federal government does not recognize the category socially maladjusted in special education, but states are free to use it, e.g., New Jersey). This is a very real problem because the stresses of poverty place greater demands on psychological adjustment, with the end result being that the poor are punished twice — both in the neighborhood with the day to day struggle to survive, and at school with the generally excessive and rigid demands for conformity to standards of more affluent-type mild-mannered behavior and academic achievement.

There are far more students classified emotionally disturbed (ED) and socially maladjusted (SM) in poor areas, especially in the cities, than there are in the more comfortable suburban or semi-rural areas. The reason for this is twofold. Firstly, the social and adjustment problems of the poor are more serious. Secondly, the more affluent and better educated parents would not usually accept their children being labeled SM or ED by the schools. The children of the affluent, legally sophisticated who are in special education have for years, in many cases, been labeled as learning disabled (LD) instead of ED, SM, or EMR because school officials fear possible law suits from them if the more noxious labels are given to their children. In addition, the suburban child labeled ED often has a more mild condition than the poor urban ED youngster. This situation can be referred to as the 'cultural relativity phenomenon' inherent in special educational labeling.

Current LD Concerns

The Weak Conceptual Basis: Theory And Practice

Since it can be said that Strauss and Werner were the fathers of the contemporary pre-LD period based on their work of the late 1930s to early 1940s, so too can it be said that Seymour B. Sarason — a psychologist who has made a career of criticizing the follies of education and professional psychology — is the period's first critic. Sarason's (1949) complaint can be summarized as follows:

> Diagnosis of a child as exogenous (brain injured) rather than endogenous (non brain injured) on the basis of behavioral manifestations led Strauss and Werner into a circular argument when they asserted that the same behaviors were the result of brain damage. (Cruickshank and Hallahan, 1973, p. 324)

Alan O. Ross (1977) had this incisive commentary on the pre-LD work:

> Because the work of Strauss and Werner was to have a major influence on those who later came to think about children with learning disabilities, it is well to point to the logical flaw in their reasoning. Adults who are presumed to have been normal prior to

their brain injury seem to have trouble with figure-ground perception. It does not necessarily follow from this that retarded children who have trouble with figure-ground perception owe their retardation to brain damage. In the absence of an indication of brain damage it is fallacious to identify a child as brain injured merely on the basis of the observation that his behavior on a psychological test is similar to behavior manifested by brain-injured adults. A previously intact adult brain that has been damaged is very likely to function differently from the developing brain of a child. Even if the child's brain has sustained some damage, it is quite unlike that inflicted by the devastation wrought by a piece of shrapnel. That neither the adult war casualty nor the mentally retarded child can tell us very much about a normal child who is learning disabled would nowadays appear obvious. (p. 20)

Along these same lines, here is one other opinion:

As contrasted with adults who experience brain damage, lesions occurring early produce a sequence of responses and a reorganization of the system. Injury to a brain that is already developed has very different consequences than injury that has been sustained before the development of the ego. (Abrams, 1984, p. 30)

Thus, even in the pre-LD period, there was controversy regarding the inferential notion of brain damage in children.

When we examine the federal government's current definition of LD, we see that it explicitly attributes specific problems in learning to one or more faulty psychological processes — this line of thinking is based primarily on the work of Samuel A. Kirk. Lester Mann (1979) more or less equates these psychological processes as a reincarnated, modern and veiled version of the antiquated 'faculty psychology' which he believes emanates from the work of the great Rene Descartes (1596-1650). Faculty psychology is a 'theory that the mind is made up of separate and independent areas of power, each of which can be strengthened by exercise' (Wolman, 1973, p. 139). Mann (1971a, 1971b), therefore, takes the position that process training — perceptual training and perceptual-motor training — is useless except in extreme cases. The work of Arter and Jenkins (1977, 1979) strongly reinforces Mann's position. Recall that many in the 'remediation stage', especially at the later end, circa 1960 and beyond, advocated process (or modality — visual, auditory, tactile, kinesthetic, multimodal) training. Also consider that the lead article in the first LD journal was written by the major contemporary advocate of process training, Ray Barsch (1963, 1966, 1967, 1968). Finally, regarding such process training, the 'safest conclusion we can reach is that it is premature to draw any definitive conclusions regarding the efficacy of perceptual-motor training' (Hallahan and Cruickshank, 1973, p. 210).

The premise for the acceptance of process training consists of a threefold assumption. (a) Normal children display relatively even development in all areas. (b) Weak areas of development or psychological processes can be remediated. (c) By remediating the faulty process or processes, academic achievement will be improved. When the Advanced Study Institute formulated a more 'educationally useful LD definition' (found in this work in Chapter 3), it stressed the *discrepancy* 'between expected and actual achievement in one or more areas' which was to be determined through 'accepted' educational and psychological tests (Kass and Myklebust, 1969, p. 39). This discrepancy notion institutionalized the threefold assumption regarding process training.

Standardized achievement tests were used to measure current academic grade levels, while psychological processes were assessed by intelligence scales and perceptual tests. Two comprehensive, early, and widely used tests for the assessment of children's psychological processes are the ITPA, Experimental Edition (McCarthy and Kirk, 1961), and the WISC (Wechsler, 1949). They were followed by updated versions: the WISC-R (Wechsler, 1974), and the ITPA, Revised Edition (Kirk, McCarthy, and Kirk, 1968). Both the revised ITPA and the WISC-R contain twelve subtests which are said to reveal intrapsychic deviation from the theoretical normal and *one's own* mean score. Although the Wechsler tests can point out faulty psychological processes, they are primarily used to determine IQ and are most often administered by school psychologists. The ITPA, on the other hand, is an instrument more often used by learning consultants to find dysfunctional psychological processes. As such, we now turn our attention to it and related issues.

The major approach in the attempt to remediate any learning disability, since the formal LD inception of 1962, has been the 'diagnostic-prescriptive' (DP) model. With this approach, weak psychological processes are determined through perceptual tests — such as the ITPA. Once determined, the weak processes are then strengthened via prescribed perceptual or perceptual-motor practice and/or by the most closely related academic-like tasks. The revised edition of the ITPA contains perceptual subtests which were 'designed to isolate defects in . . . three processes of communication' for 'remediation directed to the specific areas of defective functioning' (Kirk, McCarthy, and Kirk, 1968, p. 13) that are assumed to be related to schoolwork. Only two ITPA subtests have been found to be related to academics, and regarding them: 'It seems likely that the Grammatic Closure and Auditory Association subtests measure the child's ability to use syntactic and semantic redundancy, respectively, and that this accounts for their prominence in predicting reading ability' (Sedlak and Weener, 1973, p. 149). The ITPA generally is not used today except by the earliest learning disabilities specialists. Other perceptual tests, similar to the ITPA in intent which also have questionable validity (Coles, 1978), are being utilized to classify students as LD. Yet, the diagnostic-prescriptive approach is still a common practice model.

Little more than a decade ago, Hallahan and Cruickshank (1973) attributed conceptual problems to the LD field's short history. 'Its sudden emergence as a full-blown area within special education has resulted in a vacuum of essential knowledge regarding basic constructs' (p. 271). Today, theoretical problems remain, and practical problems are getting worse.

The winds of the soft sciences are again gently blowing in another direction. Today, the new trend is more toward strongly advocating directly teaching the curriculum to LD youngsters while assuming that process training is a useless activity. Not that curricular material was not also taught to LD students earlier when advocating process training was more popular, but the diagnostic-prescriptive model is now beginning to be seriously challenged (see Ysseldyke and Algozzine, 1982). Teaching the curriculum to LD pupils, without the 'benefit' of first determining their 'specific areas of defective process functioning' (in ITPA-like terminology), is known as 'direct instruction' and has been greatly popularized recently by Douglas Carnine (1979). In 'The newer practice model' subchapter of Chapter 3 it was pointed out that the professional practice cutting edge of education connects academic remediation to special education (as portrayed by recent publication titles) along with learning strategy skills (as typified by the LD institutes). There is a movement of knowledgeable professional research-educators to dissociate themselves from LD when it is used as an educational arrangement by the public schools because the cold chill of its discomfort is being felt as a warning of the forthcoming storm of major controversy.

Rampant LD Labeling

Even though it has never been definitely proven that the so-called mild LD student learns more in separate LD classes, more and more are being labeled and segregated. Moreover, even those students classified LD who are not placed in self-contained special classes are stigmatized before they are given additional academic help through 'special' supplemental instruction or resource room type programs (see Table 3, Chapter 2). There is no reason students who need such additional programs should not be allowed to attend them without first being formally labeled, except that when they are classified as 'special' their local school districts are reimbursed by the states with federal special education funds (Sigmon, 1984 d). Supplemental and resource room programs for the non-classified are rare, and regular remedial programs funded by local boards of education are generally meager in scope. Some states, instead of using the federal government's 'special learning disabilities' tag, use their own, more antiquated labeling schema. New Jersey, for instance, has 'perceptually impaired' (PI) and 'neurologically impaired' (NI) instead of the LD label; but both categories are subsumed within the federal LD figures. NI denotes a more severe condition than PI, although students can be labeled NI and placed in self-contained NI classes without any real, 'hard' evidence of neurological disorganization, i.e., 'soft signs'.

The meek warning over the non-efficacious nature of EMR classes for the higher functioning mildly retarded was sounded first by Blatt (1960) and Johnson (1962) approximately a decade before the first court papers were filed in 1972 for the now classic Larry P. case. Dunn's (1968) warning about EMR classes, published a few years later, was the loudest and most well known to that time and possibly today as well. Perhaps the first serious formal battlelines regarding LD were formed in 1974 with Divoky's (1974) piece entitled 'Education's latest victim: The "LD" kid'. Several years later there appeared Algozzine and Sutherland's (1977) article, 'Non-psycho-educational foundations of learning disabilities' in the *Journal of Special Education*. These two pioneering publications, critical of LD classes, had virtually no impact. A year later Coles (1978), in the *Harvard Educational Review*, questioned the validity of the actual test battery utilized to classify a student LD. McKnight (1982) doubted the very existence of the LD syndrome and stated its population consisted mainly of former EMR-type youngsters. Collins and Camblin (1983) believe being formally classified LD is equally as harmful to black students as was the EMR rubric. The crisis is fomenting, and it is only a matter of time until the first potentially (in)famous LD court case begins.

As it turns out, McKnight was correct. The LD and EMR populations are doing a flip-flop in terms of numbers (see Table 4). Many of the same type of child who was formerly classified EMR is probably now a candidate for the LD classification. Table 4 graphically depicts the dramatic increase in the formally classified LD population. From the 1976–77 schoolyear to that of 1982–83, LD students have more than doubled in number. During these same six schoolyears, the national mentally retarded group has shrunk by almost 20 per cent. The US Department of Education does not differentiate among the mild, moderate, and severely retarded. However, it would be

Table 4[1]: Total US special education students ages 3–21 by selected federal categories for schoolyears 1976 to 1983[2]

Schoolyear	Specific learning disability	Mentally retarded[3]	Seriously emotionally disturbed	Total by year (All conditions[4])
1976–77	797,213	969,547	283,072	3,708,588
1977–78	969,423	944,980	288,634	3,777,286
1978–79	1,135,559	917,880	301,469	3,919,073
1979–80	1,281,379	882,173	331,067	4,036,219
1980–81	1,468,014	844,180	348,954	4,177,689
1981–82	1,627,344	802,264	341,786	4,233,282
1982–83	1,745,871	780,831	353,431	4,298,327

[1]Adapted by author from US Office of Special Education (1983, Appendix 2, Table F, pp. 72, 74, 76, 90; and, 1984, Table 3A6, pp. 136–137, 139–140).
[2]Figures include 1700 students from US possessions of American Samoa, Guam, Northern Marianas, and the Virgin Islands in 1982–83.
[3]The federal Department of Education is not required by law to distinguish levels of retardation in its annual report to Congress.
[4]Conditions omitted from this table are speech impaired, other health impaired, multihandicapped, hard of hearing, deaf, orthopedically impaired, visually handicapped, and deaf-blind.

safe to conjecture that probably the moderate and definitely the severe retardate populations — over whom there has been little real controversy, and should not be — are relatively stable in relation to the general population. We can also suppose that many or even most of the mildly intellectually/academically impaired, who in the past would have been initially labeled EMR, are now instead first labeled LD. The question that remains is: Why has the LD group more than doubled while the EMR population has shrunk by only approximately 20 per cent? The answer is twofold. (a) The mildly retarded population already classified will in most cases dissipate only through attrition (graduation) as they will remain classified EMR unless very strong objections are raised regarding their present status. And (b), the overall national special education population is growing, and most of this growth is found in the LD category. The US Department of Education has provided to Congress by legal mandate the figures on the national special education population since PL94–142 went into effect during the 1977–78 schoolyear; and since that time, more than 600,000 additional children have been formally classified. Simultaneously with the LD-EMR flip-flop, there has been growth of approximately 25 per cent in the labeled American emotionally disturbed (ED) group. There is no doubt that a sizable number of these ED students have real and serious personal problems. However, many within this ED category probably exhibit a learning profile similar in nature to the mild LD's; but the ED youngster is often less remorseful over poor achievement, is usually less concerned with school decorum, and might be more active at school.

There are now in America over $4\frac{1}{4}$-million schoolchildren who are formally classified as being educationally handicapped of whom 41 per cent are labeled LD (based on US Office of Special Education, 1984). The probable trend is for both to increase. Since it is believed here that the federal government's broad definition of LD tacitly allows for the classification of children with no actual physiological disability, it stands to reason that many of the LD students are considered to be 'mildly educationally handicapped' due to social/academic problems. Moreover, because most of the students classified LD really comprise an under-achieving group who are problematic in terms of traditional rigid grade level groupings, 'Few findings describe the types of children who are being identified as learning disabled' (Comptroller General of the United States, 1981, p. iii). Furthermore, 'of the children receiving special education, 13 percent were classified as having severe handicaps, 36 percent as moderate handicaps, and 51 percent as mild handicaps' (p. 20); and 'A "typical" child in special education is under 12 years of age, male, and mildly handicapped' (Comptroller General of the United States, 1981, front cover). Other uncomfortable statistics were found which strongly suggest that special education has become the means for containing the types of children which general American public education cannot effectively deal with in regular programs, i.e., those who are not white females from English speaking homes. See the Comptroller General's (1981) findings following:

> Forty-one percent of black students in special education programs in school year 1978 were in classes for the educable mentally retarded as compared with only ten percent of Asian American students receiving special education and 17 percent of Hispanic students receiving services. Almost one half of the American Indian students in special education programs in the public schools were in learning disabled classes in 1978. Fifty percent of Asian Americans in special education were in speech impaired programs in 1978. (p. iii) Males are three times as likely as females to be found in programs for the seriously emotionally disturbed. Males are two and one half times as likely as females to be in learning disabled programs. (p. iv)

This is cruel madness. How many more children — with alleged mild disorders of all kinds, or members of groups incompatible with the rigid general public school grade level system — will be led to believe that there is within themselves something wrong before this cruel hoax, the latter 20th century American special education travesty against children, comes to an end?

The Reproduction-Resistance Dialectic

Social Class, Ideology, and Education

The functionalist sociologists of education were described as those who seek to justify and preserve the existing social order. A prime example of this is that of Warner, Havighurst, and Loeb's (1944) discussion of 'basic social problems and social issues of our society' and the content of their 'proposed educational program':

> It should aim to teach an approach to social problems which all American citizens can adopt and which will help them to deal with their inevitable clashes of economic interest in ways which will maintain cooperation among the various social and economic groups in the nation. (p. 159)

The new sociologists of education also study the relationship of sociology to education but do not necessarily seek harmony and consensus for the preservation of the status quo — as they recognize the need for social change due to the contradiction between democratic theory and practice in the postindustrial capitalist state. This radical position is based on conflict theory.

Hurn (1978) was certainly correct when he wrote that there are 'ideological barriers to clear thought about schools' (p. 20). Bourdieu and Passeron (1977) believe there is often 'blindness to the relations between the school and the social classes, as if ascertaining the fact of autonomy presupposed the illusion of the educational system's neutrality' (p. 195). The educational system in the United States, although allowing and even encouraging some creativity and criticism — primarily at the tertiary level — is a primary means of conserving the existing culture and dominant class interests. (Creativity, criticism, and conservation are the three Cs of education). Special education, perhaps more than any other component of the educational system, is influenced by psychology; and mainstream, establishment psychology is, for the most part, ideologically linked to the dominant culture.

> In class society, the dominant views, ideology and philosophy are those of the dominant class. Since the social and behavioral sciences are of great influence in the formation of the ideology and beliefs in capitalist society, these sciences cannot be viewed as pure sciences, separated from social or class interests. They must be analyzed as being also shaped, influenced, and distorted by the class which controls the government, the educational and university system, the

commercial media, and the wealth to subsidize specific views and ideology. Hence, psychology cannot be viewed as a neutral science, unaffected by class interests. (Nahem, 1981, p. 13)

Liberals show concern for the plight of the individual doing poorly within America; and they attempt to slowly modify, reform, and bring about the realization of democracy via the schools — but this has not worked. The destitute individual, from the conservative viewpoint, is merely of inferior biological stock and reproduces other, similar persons and therefore reform is useless. Ironically, both the conservative and the radical see piecemeal reform as ultimately useless; but whereas the former wants no change at all, the latter seeks major change. The radical position is that the root source of many social problems in America lies in the simultaneity of political freedom and economic inequality, including those found in the schools. The schools mirror cultural problems as a whole. Education, or more specifically schooling, is designed to prevent real change because it is charged with preserving dominant class interests within the culture. The structure of American schooling has not really changed. The 'crisis in American education' is really the crisis of American society at large. Special education, over the past twenty years or so, has become co-opted; and this use of it is actually an attempt at reform *from within* to salvage the failures of society at large outside the schools. Unless major social changes are made in the arena of economic equality, the problems of the schools obviously will never be rectified.

Class Interests, School Goals, and Student Resisters

It must be understood that 'as education became a state function, instruction was bent increasingly to serve the ends of the state' (Lucas, 1972, p. 393). Furthermore, the state is the actual manifestation of the political ideology — which can and will use violence via the police and the courts to suppress dissent when found to be excessively threatening to the existing social order — that allows certain economic institutions to exist. 'In Prussia, for example, the first major educational efforts of the early nineteenth century, . . . were initiated with the avowed aim of fostering state patriotism' (Lucas, 1972, p. 393). Orthodox Marxists, and others, often mistakenly believe(d) that the state can in its schools correspondingly reproduce within its students, in a straightforward manner, a certain desired ideological type of consciousness. The reproduction theory was earlier generally posited in the literature via economic examples with 'the school as a figurative factory in which student-workers produced knowledge-commodities under the direction of teacher-foremen' (Curtis, 1984, p. 42). Although Bowles and Gintis (1976) adhered to the reproduction theory, they advanced it in their analysis of 'the contradictions of economic life'. In his *Selections from the prison notebooks*, Antonio Gramsci (1941/1971):

> rejects the view that the superstructure is a simple reflection of the economic base. Gramsci believes there is a constantly changing reciprocal relationship between culture and economics. He introduced the concept of 'hegemony' to explain how the ruling class uses a system of beliefs, values and attitudes in all areas of life as a means of *legitimizing* itself. Revolutionary education would entail the *demystifying* of the dominant beliefs and values of capitalist education, and the development of a *counter-hegemony* in order to establish a new set of meanings and values. (D'Angelo, 1982, pp. 136–137)

The schools are capable of this sort of ideological reproduction, but their success in doing so is uneven. Children are far from being passive reservoirs for the school's doctrine. This author believes that the school's ability to inculcate the dominant view is basically dependent upon the student's level of alienation — in the Marxian sense — which is almost always developed outside of school. Abject poverty, knowledge of chronic unemployment, or familiarity of militant trade unionism in poor homes are likely causes of conscious alienation, while children and youths from more affluent homes are often alienated by hypocritical and biased government policies.

It is possible for a rather alienated pupil to do well in school academically without internalizing the dominant ideological line. However, it is quite likely that the alienated student will refuse to do much schoolwork. Such a student is not scholastically motivated, and will herein be described as a *school resister*. It is proposed that many student resisters have been formally classified with various special education labels such as emotionally disturbed, socially maladjusted, and especially learning disabled — because LD is the easiest one to assign a student since it is the least noxious — by a general education system unable to deal with them. (There is a trend now by states that still use clinical labels to switch to descriptive labels, e.g., a speech deficit or LD becomes a communicative disorder; but regardless of the type of labeling system, if school resisters are placed in special education, the end result is the same). These children are victims on the school front of a diffuse, and still in most quarters, unconscious and undeclared social class war. The functional sociologists of education recommend a particular educational program specifically designed to avoid 'inevitable clashes of economic interest' (Warner *et al.*, 1944) which actually attempts to indoctrinate students in the belief that the current American politicoeconomic structure should remain the same because this is in everyone's best interests. The schools are the institutions charged with the mission of transmitting this belief regarding the viability and righteousness of the current superstructure. The schools can stretch as they must to implement this sort of propagandistic educational program; but like an elastic band, the schools will spring back to their original posture or flex again to accommodate new resistance. The student resisters are not handicapped as per the original and still valid intent of special education — which is to serve well the moderately to profoundly disabled. It is also thought that many of the resisters classified as LD do not even qualify under the federal government's own specific learning disabilities definition because 'The term does not include children . . . of environmental, cultural, or economic disadvantage'.

As more and more socioeconomically disenfranchised children enter school, if things remain as they are, these children will continue to be unconscionably added to the already burgeoning special education population. Additionally, the older alienated youths, many of whom live in urban areas, will drop out of school and commit much of the rising violent city crime which will necessitate the building of many more prisons. The reproduction-resistance dialectic is a way of understanding the class struggle and education. Although a number of recent, prominent studies on American education publicized the crisis in the schools, they did not really recognize that social class struggle is the major root problem.

Interactionism: Basis for Theory and Rational Educational Intervention

When a child is not doing well in school and is found to be educationally handicapped because of a particular medical condition or corresponding clinical educational category, the deficit, defect, or medical model has been applied. In this way, the problem is seen as emanating from within the child, i.e., the problem is physiologically internal or psychologically intrapsychic. The defect model is not really unsound with severe or even possibly moderate disorders, especially those of actual, identifiable physiological genesis. However, when supposed mild disorders are assumed on the basis of inferential data in conjunction with poor school achievement and/or a lack of conformity to school rules, the defect model becomes less rational and more suspect.

Hobbs (1975), in his noted critical study about classification and special education, issued a plea for a new 'proposed model for classifying' in which 'a profile of assets and liabilities describes the transactions between the child and people significant in his life, always in particular settings and at particular times' (p. 105). Once the profile is developed, it becomes 'the basis for specification of treatment objectives and of time limits for accomplishing goals agreed upon by all who are party to their realization' (Hobbs, 1975, p. 105). Hobbs' notion is primitive but humane as its purpose was to de-emphasize formal labeling and to limit its use over time with individual students when possible. However, his attention to 'transactions' and 'particular settings' was a positive step in moving away from the intrapsychic defect model with the mildly handicapped youngster which had by 1975 become so controversial — especially for the EMR label.

When Algozzine and Sutherland (1977) wrote about 'non-psycho-educational foundations of LD', they were specifically addressing the social — as opposed to the intrapsychic — origins of the learning problem. They felt that few LD children were 'physically afflicted' with any real medical deficit. They listed three major fallacious underlying assumptions inherent, by and large, to the LD field: (a) 'There is . . . a state of psychoeducational health which can be adequately diagnosed and remediated', (b) 'School success' yields 'life success and happiness', and (c), 'All children are equally motivated toward achievement of socially derived goals fostered by education' (p. 95). Refuted by them therefore is the underlying process disorder notion. Additionally, even though Algozzine and Sutherland mentioned that 'many scholars would argue that the schooling process is essentially a politically expeditious enterprise, working to the detriment of many of its clients' (p. 93), they left us only with the admonition to 'look at the interactive nature of student-teacher relationships and academic learning' (p. 97). The same sort of view is espoused by Senf (1981) with his 'learner-system interactions' whereby 'dehandicapping' children forms the basis of his 'child-school interaction model'. The recent learning disability institutes, circa 1977 to 1982 (see Kneedler and Hallahan, 1983), also to a great extent emphasized interaction which is the rationale for what this author calls the 'newer practice model'.

The current federal LD definition, as found in PL94–142, has produced a witch hunt of sorts within the public schools. Mann *et al.* (1983) — referring to the circa 1971 to 1980 Child Service Demonstration Centers, which had different constituencies and various interpretations of the first federal definition of LD (by the National Advisory Committee on Handicapped Children, 1968) — wrote that 'Any consensus on the definition of LD, if indeed one ever existed, has, of course, dissipated since 1971' (p. 16). This writer takes the position that all the LD definitions ever formulated — despite their apparent excessive inclusiveness — are all definitions by exclusion. Hence, if a child cannot fit any of the other special education definitions, there looms large the possibility the student is classifiable as LD if achievement in even one scholastic area is low. Special education has been, inappropriately and unfortunately, relegated the task of solving the problems of a failing general education system. Moreover, if things stay as they are, special education's problem solving role will increase while general education will be able to accommodate fewer and fewer regular education students. A simultaneous increase in vocational education is probably also helping to keep afloat a leaky-hulled educational system at the secondary level.

Learning disabilities as a field really originated from psychology, medicine, and mental retardation as a result of work with brain damaged (retarded) children. Developing better methods of educating brain damaged children, both retarded and those who were intellectually normal — especially the cerebral palsied, even in their own separate classes — made a great deal of sense. However, as the intact children started being classified LD and were placed in special classes, both psychology and education subtly became perverted. Medical science and special educational methods were the reasons given by naive but well intentioned school officials for this practice which led to the extraordinarily rapid expansion of LD programs. Virtually none of the research on LD students, with the exception of the interactional variety typical of the LD institutes, is valid, as it mistakenly discusses many dissimilar LD children as if they were a homogeneous grouping which they cannot possibly be because of the broad definitions.

While much of this present work has been devoted to making a case of the social rather than biological causes of LD — other radical educational writings also attribute social factors to various other educational problems — socialist and 'Soviet researchers, unlike their American counterparts, are not interested in *proving* the role that the social environment plays in learning. Instead, they begin with unquestioned acceptance of this role' (Gibson, 1984, p. 93). Moreover, 'Marxist dialectical philosophy suggests that higher-order mental processes develop through direct interaction with the environment. . . . Soviet research therefore involves demonstrating *how* the social environment affects learning and what manipulation of the environment produces maximal desired learning' (Gibson, 1984, p. 93). The American education policy making establishment (which is really Congress) and influential professional educators, should they recognize the real social causes of learning problems in the schools (the existing socioeconomic arrangements), which seems unlikely in the near future, could reverse the existing LD dilemma with an interactional approach to education.

The Soviet Union is said to have a long history of well established programs for handicapped youngsters, but only relatively recently has research and practice been instituted there for those having 'temporarily retarded psychological development' (TRPD) which is the closest Soviet equivalent to LD (Wozniak, 1975). Not surprisingly, the Soviets view TRPD 'as developing within interactive social relationships' (Coles, 1983, p. 619) which is quite different from the biological reductionist account of LD generally posited as causative by most American proponents, especially those in the public schools. Contradistinctively, there is an emerging trend for research and applied psychology in America to utilize the interactional approach (see Sigmon, 1984 a, 1984 b). Hopefully, this socially more realistic trend in American psychology at large will provide legitimacy for application of the interactional model to general education in the United States. When this occurs, special education will no longer inappropriately be a means of child control.

Interactionism — as it affects education and how it has been implicitly discussed — can be viewed at both the micro- and macro-system levels. The microlevel involves exchanges between teachers and students in various school settings; i.e., actual social interactional patterns, instructional methodology, curricula, and school programs. The larger, superstructure level (or the socio-political system) is concerned with what happens outside of school. The macrosystem, therefore, deals with social class arrangements, and this, perhaps more than anything else, affects what occurs in schools (Sigmon, 1985 a). When seen in this light — as Young (1971) intimated — both levels can and should be studied as well as changed, in more humane ways, simultaneously.

Summary

The LD controversy of the 1980s follows on the heels of the EMR disputation of the 1970s. Actually, the earlier EMR dispute created, in many ways, the present controversial LD situation. In as much as the EMR label is primarily determined via IQ testing, in relation to academic achievement, IQ tests were scrutinized by the courts during significant litigation pertaining to them during the 1970s. The courts found that intelligence scales were biased against ethnic minorities, most of whom are poor, and therefore decreed that their use be de-emphasized for EMR placements. Moreover, this author has reached the conclusion that *no* cognitive test is culturally fair, by and large, to socioeconomically depressed students no matter how innocent the test may appear.

With social pressure against EMR label usage, the number of EMR students has decreased, while the use of the somewhat less noxious LD classification has increased dramatically. With so many students now considered LD, methods and rationales regarding this practice require careful examination. Brain damage and the more recent notion of faulty internal psychological processes are spurious rationales for the labeling of most LD children who are said to have only mild handicaps. Furthermore, the thinking regarding these dysfunctional processes for the mildly disabled LD youngster is akin to charlatanism. Such youngsters are merely low achievers, who are not being properly taught — despite better teaching methodology which has been developed — (Steven A. Carlson, personal communication, June 28, 1984), or school resisters (Linda Gonzalves, personal communication, April 3, 1984).

After having traced what led to the LD controversy, a radical socio-educational analysis of it reveals several important points. There are conceptual problems with the LD notion as it applies to most children so labeled which leads to inappropriate educational arrangements for them and counterproductive attitudes about the way they learn. The result of current practice is that the LD label is used as a means of child control in the schools, and as a way of gaining additional funds to pay for programs after children are stigmatized. Finally, it must be recognized that the increasing number of LD children represents social and economic problems outside the schools, and these problems signify an ongoing social class struggle.

Chapter 5

Closing

The philosophers have *interpreted* the world in various ways; the point however is to *change* it.
Karl Marx (1845/1941, p. 84)

Introduction

This chapter asks: What are the implications of a radical socioeducational analysis (RSA) for American special education, the LD controversy, and future practice and policy? This complex question will be addressed within the two major subchapters that follow. The first is basically a summation, while the second looks at policy and future practice.

Discussion of Radical Analysis

History

When we turn to the history of American special education we see a constant macrosociological dialectic in process. That is, there is on the one hand the humanitarian desire to provide the handicapped with the finest education possible. Yet, on the other, special education has compensated for the inadequacies of general education and has had to compete with it for a finite amount of funds. Additionally, although there were several residential institutions established for the instruction of the severely handicapped in the first half of the 19th century in Massachusetts and Connecticut — for the blind, 'deaf and dumb', the 'feebleminded', and 'socially maladjusted' — it was not until regular education was made compulsory, between 1852 and 1918, in the various states, that special education would later become significant. The factors of social class bias and racial prejudice delayed the establishment of free mass public compulsory general education in the

United States; but when it was established, special education later accommodated those who did not fit in.

There are three basic models for educating the handicapped: special residential and day schools, special classes in regular schools, and partial special educational programming combined with regular classes which is known as mainstreaming. Mainstreaming is a dual edged concept as it allows some handicapped pupils to be in a more normalized program; but it also can be used to deprive truly handicapped youngsters of needed services to save local school districts money if these services are not fully funded by state governments via federal reimbursement. It is best to meet all of an exceptional child's needs, but this must be done with as little stigmatization, labeling, and segregation as possible. Obviously, the more handicapped the child, the more restrictive the educational setting must be and more specialized services (e.g., physical therapy) must be provided.

The initial students in special education, by and large, were those with physical and sensory handicaps. Not surprisingly, the most severely impaired became the responsibility of the local school districts last. Many special classes for the retarded were set up in regular public schools in the cities during the first half of the twentieth century, and so were a few for the socially maladjusted. An extremely large number of students were placed in EMR special classes — even though a sizable number were more handicapped by culture, especially language, than intellectual deficits.

Due to the advent of the great Depression, 'from 1930 to 1940 there was a halt and even a decline in' the special class 'trend' (Robinson and Robinson, 1965, p. 460). However, the demographics of the 1950s and early 1960s presented a unique set of circumstances. The baby-boom following World War II was in full swing. As a result, parents' groups had become large plus influential, and were demanding much from education — including special facilities for their handicapped children and special classes were again promoted enthusiastically (Robinson and Robinson, 1965). This was to become an extremely productive professional period in special education with a concomitant receptive public. The year 1957 marked the beginning of federal financial support for special education whereupon $667,000 was earmarked for the education of the retarded (PL85–531, 'Cooperative research act'; see Table 2 in Chapter 2). With the US government becoming involved with education for the handicapped the stage was set for special education's massive growth and national legalized institutionalization.

We have already been made aware of and warned about children formally labeled and placed in special, segregated educational programs by many writers. In certain cases this may be best for the individual student because of the severity of the learning problem. Earlier intense debates on special education have focused on those children classified as mildly or educable mentally retarded (EMR) (Blatt, 1960; Dunn, 1968; G.O. Johnson, 1962; just to list the earlier major protagonists), deviant (behaviored) or socially maladjusted (J.L. Johnson, 1969; *et al.*), and emotionally disturbed (e.g., Rubin, Simson, and Betwee, 1966). Learning disability is actually the newest key category in special education, and we are now confronted with serious issues regarding it.

LD Concept

When examining the genesis and institutionalization of LD through RSA, root cultural influences — unlike the functional approach which merely offers 'objective' historical facts — are stressed. For instance, it has already been discussed how special schools and special classes evolved, but it was really the scientific 'child study' movement started by G. Stanley Hall (1883, 1900, 1901–2) around the turn of this century which produced in American culture the mental set whereby individual differences were to be greatly considered when schooling youngsters. One of Hall's most famous students, Lewis M. Terman, greatly popularized in the USA the IQ test which was the primary 'scientific' means for legitimizing classes for the mildly retarded. This led America to voluntary but also *mandated* classes — the latter type were first located in New Jersey during 1911 — for the so-called educationally retarded. Yet, there is no doubt that IQ tests are biased against the poor and the culturally different. (It is noteworthy that there was no formal category for the mildly retarded person before the advent of various grade levels). Next, specialized remedial reading appeared in the 1920s (Smith, 1961). The mid-1930s began the 'slow learner' period (Ingram, 1935/1960) which — although greatly forgotten and ignored, the concept is still taught to graduate special education students — maintained and built momentum into the 1960s (G.O. Johnson, 1963; Kephart, 1960; Younie, 1967). The slow learner, a vague term with various parameters, can be consensually defined as being a student who is not retarded but achieves below the 50 percentile — although achievement is usually quite lower and IQ can be as low as borderline retarded. A major contention of this work is that those topics found within this paragraph helped prepare the path for the institutionalization of LD as a separate educational track. This is because categorizing, special teaching, and educationally segregating schoolchildren were accepted as standard practice, and new tests and categories would further facilitate this practice.

Regardless of one's research paradigm or point of view about LD, the strong early influence of physicians, especially neurologists, cannot be denied. The same can be said about the work of Alfred A. Strauss and Heinz Werner, but especially that of Samuel A. Kirk. However, Strauss and Werner, who were most influential in the contemporary pre-LD period, and Kirk, the father of the modern LD stage, have come under attack in some quarters recently. (This will be looked at in the next section). Therefore, we should review their ideas regarding the roots of the LD concept.

Shortly after World War I in Germany the neurologist Kurt Goldstein studied the aftereffects of brain injuries sustained by German soldiers. Goldstein's soldiers had difficulty with abstractions, were incapable of differentiating between figure and ground, stimulus bound, prone to catastrophic reactions, perseverative, meticulous, and orderly (Ross, 1977). While still in Germany, young Strauss, a neuropsychiatrist, studied under Goldstein. After having emigrated to the USA, Strauss was teamed up with Werner, another young German emigré and an already noted developmental psychologist, at the Wayne County Training School in Northville, MI, in 1937. This was a progressive residential school for educable mentally retarded students which, under very enlightened leadership and a generous budget, also conducted research of high caliber and trained graduate psychology students from the University of Michigan (William M. Cruickshank, personal communication, March 8, 1984). Strauss, while at this training school, which served Detroit and no longer exists, was known as an 'idea man' (Cruickshank, personal communication, March 15, 1984). In the late 1930s, Strauss (1938) had become seriously interested in 'exogenous factors' as causative to 'mental deficiency' in children, and this later led to the establishment of two distinct categories of retardation: those whose retardation is a result of external brain insult or the 'exogenous type', and those without 'brain damage' (familial retardation) or the 'endogenous type' (Martinson and Strauss, 1940). And so the connection to the earlier war victims: 'Goldstein and Gelb have described a disturbance in the differentiation of figure and background in brain-injured adult patients. We have attempted, in various experimental situations, to demonstrate the presence of this disturbance in *brain-injured children*' (Werner and Strauss, 1940, p. 440, emphasis added). Although new work by Werner and Strauss continued to be published into the 1950s and 1960s, their major contributions to special education were really highlighted in a classic book entitled *Psychopathology and education of the brain-injured child* (Strauss and Kephart, 1955).

Kirk, although stating 'I did not originate the term "specific learning disability"' (Kirk, 1976, p. 257), was the first known writer to use the terms 'specific learning disability' in a book (Kirk, 1962) and 'learning disabilities' in a journal article (Kirk and Bateman, 1962). In Kirk's (1962) lengthy textbook, his section on 'Learning disabilities' comprised less than twelve full pages, with only slightly more than two pages covering an explicit discussion of LD, all of which was found at the end of chapter ten (of fourteen) entitled 'Cerebral palsy and associated disorders'. It is one of the major ironies of the special education literature that the Kirk and Bateman (1962) article appeared in the same issue of *Exceptional Children* — a leading, early special education journal still published — with the one by G.O. Johnson (1962). Johnson's piece, indeed not the first to point out the inadequacies of special EMR classes for their students (Blatt, 1960, was earlier), made the strongest case to date against them. G.O. Johnson (1962) concluded that with very mildly retarded youngsters whose average IQ was 65, 'The reported research to date does not support the subjective evaluations of teachers and their contention that the education for mentally handicapped children in special classes is superior to that provided these children in regular classes' (pp. 66–67). It is even more ironic that in the first LD article (Kirk and Bateman, 1962) even though 'training programs' and 'remedial procedures' are discussed, special claBateman, 1962) even though 'training programs' and 'remedial procedures' are discussed, special classes for the learning disabled are not. You, the reader, decide what was meant by training programs.

Kirk's intimate involvement with the field of LD is substantial in many ways — through organizations (parent and professional), with the federal government, academically, and through research and tests. It is sufficient to say that Kirk is, more than anyone else, most responsible for the establishment of the notion of LD; and interestingly, Kirk worked at the Wayne County School while a doctoral student, between 1931 and 1935, prior to the arrival in 1937 of both Strauss and Werner. Kirk (1976) suggested the term LD in 1963 to a parents' group who welcomed it and which would later become known as the Association for Children with Learning Disabilities (or ACLD). LD is obviously a much more palatable term than brain damaged, brain injured, or other phrases of that ilk, and is more educationally relevant. The nonretarded brain damaged child who was also a slow learner, and therefore needed specialized instruction, became the LD student. Hence, most original LD students either had brain damage attributable to a definite physical injury or exhibited the extreme behavior described by Strauss and Werner.

Kirk was the mentor for a dissertation which produced a pre-school psycholinguistic test (Sievers, 1955/1956). Later, he became the primary developer of a similar test for schoolchildren (ITPA) (Kirk and McCarthy, 1961). This test was for years afterwards used, in revised form, by learning disabilities specialists to diagnose LD and recommend remedial techniques. The ITPA was used to find 'discrepant abilities' among 'psychological functions' by examining communication 'processes' or 'channels' via the 'auditory-vocal and the visual-motor' 'modalities' — because the ITPA's 'purpose' was to serve as a 'diagnostic/teaching model' (Kirk, McCarthy and Kirk, 1968, pp. 5–7). The ITPA is reported to be 'a diagnostic test of specific cognitive abilities, as well as a test of molar intelligence' (Kirk *et al.*, 1968, p. 5). Recently, the ITPA has fallen out of grace because of serious questions about its validity, and is generally now used only by the oldest LD specialists. Nevertheless, the ITPA and other refined inferential perceptual/cognitive tests continue to be used to identify many other students as LD who are unlike the original severely learning disabled youngster described in 1963 when ACLD was formed.

Kirk's original LD definition and that used today by the federal government (in PL94–142) to classify children are quite similar, except that the former's is more broad and inclusive in scope. The Kirk and Bateman (1962) definition of LD was concerned with 'delayed development in one or more . . . processes resulting from a psychological handicap caused by a possible cerebral dysfunction. . . . not the result of retardation' (p. 73). By ruling out mental retardation (MR) from the learning disabilities definition, Kirk took the position that true MR youngsters were only those with low IQs who also had flat, low profiles for all subtests on all comprehensive cognitive tests.

> All the children I taught at the Wayne County Training School were classified as mentally retarded. In all of these cases my purpose was to show through the results of remediation that these children should have been classified as learning disabled instead of mentally retarded, since they were normal in some respects but had specific disabilities. (Kirk, 1976, p. 260)

Although Kirk may have helped 'rescue' to some degree a great number of children from being classified MR — the courts probably had more effect — he inadvertently constructed a new major thoroughfare into special education for millions of children.

LD Controversy

LD was not originally conceived as being a particular medical syndrome comprising a homogeneous group. Rather, it was meant to be a way of viewing a dysfunctional learning style, studied by research-educators, to help teachers instruct children.

The controversy actually began in the contemporary pre-LD period with Strauss and Werner. They took a flawed giant conceptual leap in assuming that retarded children who have difficulty with figure-ground perception and who may exhibit other behaviors similar to soldiers with head wounds, are brain damaged. Nevertheless, the same assumption was then applied to the nonretarded.

'While the research of the 1930s and 1940s had essentially been focused on mental retardation, we were trying to ascertain whether the observed characteristics with that early group also pertain to the intellectually normal' (Cruickshank, 1976, p. 105). When the thinking regarding LD became fixated on the nonretarded, LD could then more easily be used to separate youngsters.

> Without anticipating the problems to ensue, a line of demarcation was drawn between mental retardation and learning disabilities — a horizontal line separating the two groups at approximately an intellectual level of I.Q. 80. National, state, and local definitions of learning disability reflect this error. In reality the line should be drawn vertically, if indeed there should be a line at all. Essentially what we know about learning disabilities of a perceptual nature in intellectually normal children is based upon the research done with exogenous mentally retarded children. Learning disabilities are characteristic of children and youth of any chronological age and of *any and all intellectual levels*. The artifact of differentiation between the two clinical groups is just that, a recent man-made artifact. It is illogical. . . . the exclusion of the perceptually handicapped mentally retarded child from the specialized teaching and learning situations which are germane to his peculiar learning needs is an unnecessary tragedy, and the situation must be rectified quickly. That professionals permitted this situation to develop is a sad commentary. (Cruickshank, 1976, p. 106)

The IQ demarcation is the second major controversial aspect of LD. This fulfilled a cultural need for American education. That is, a 'scientific' reason was provided to explain why some children — who were not handicapped in previously thought of ways — were not learning in America's public schools. This also provided a rationale to set them aside from regular classes. Furthermore, the LD notion came along at a time when special education began to grow and to be taken much more seriously than ever before.

The third and most serious aspect of the LD controversy is that: (a) the number of children formally classified is alarming and growing, (b) most of these students are considered to have only a mild inferential disorder — they are nothing like the quite disabled original LD group who may or may not have had brain damage — and are normal in most all respects except for poor academic achievement, and (c) LD has been used as the justification for new educational arrangements which have become a massive means of social control in the schools with children and youths. There have been warnings sounded over the years about these three major controversial aspects of LD, but they went unheeded.

Two paramount factors regarding LD specifically and special education generally have been established. Low achieving youngsters and classified mildly handicapped special education students have similar learning profiles because they constitute the same basic 'client pool'. This is the root cause of the 'problem' in this study and is the reason for its pervasiveness.

Society is not really coming to the aid of many students. There are no real options today for most low achieving students, especially the poor. Remedial funds for the disadvantaged have decreased while special education has grown. PL94–142 was intended not only to insure free entitlement to special education for all who truly need it, but also to prevent students from being removed from regular education unnecessarily. Yet, the opposite has happened. PL94–142's controls were circumvented for the convenience of the schools. However, in defense of the schools, they are forced to deal with students who are *required* to attend, many of whom do not want to be there. Many students do not like what they are required to do or study. Social class values and life-styles clash at school, but the school must contain all these students. Remember, the school is charged by the larger society with the responsibility of reproducing culture but it meets resistance in doing this.

Pupils who are hard to teach have been systematically discriminated against through selective implementation of special educational placement. Those who are 'learning disinterested' (Algozzine and Sutherland, 1977) or display 'disturbingness' toward teachers (Algozzine, 1975/1976) are referred to child study teams which function as the gate-keepers to special education. The child study teams — who view themselves as child advocates — do not operate with nefarious intent. Rather, these teams place children in special education as this has become their expected major role today, and because there is little else they can do while busily adding to the special education population. Role expectations are very strong in determining behavior, but stronger still is the explicit threat by unscrupulous school administrators that certain quotas for classifying students must be reached or a team's exmployment is placed in jeopardy. Classification and placement of low achieving and disturbing children are short-term benefits for schools and teachers at the expense of long-term benefits to children. Most local special education administrators either do not understand the intent of PL94–142 or lack ethical perspectives regarding special placements. The regulations are circumvented when: school district bureaucrats seek to gain additional funds through the classification of students, child study teams inappropriately nurture students by placing them in special education for lack of other options, and the school as an institution uses special education for veiled disciplinary purposes.

Some believe that the other factors which drive the engine to classification are poor teaching, the climate of professional organizations such as teachers' unions, and the rapid implementation of PL94–142 which institutionalized incompetence among those who work in special education in the public schools. This may be true to some extent, but this writer believes that this attitude unfairly blames public school workers for special education's sad state.

Inappropriate perceptual and cognitive tests are still used in support of the diagnostic-prescriptive (DP) or discrepancy model to identify students with alleged mild LD. The DP model — which attempts to measure faulty communicative psychological processes — favored by Kirk and others of similar persuasion is not an efficacious way of viewing students, yet it became extremely popular. What is the DP model's attraction and why did it gain so strong a following? Why was Kirk's group — and not Englemann's, which advocated the more effective applied behavioral analysis (ABA) model — listened to? The DP model represents a theory of convenience that works in the interests of teachers and schools.

We know there are other things we can and should do but do not. For instance, there could be more pre-referral consultation and intervention prior to the formal referral which usually leads to special education placement. In addition, the sophisticated technology of teaching, the ABA model, and direct instruction that have been developed should be used on a much wider scale.

It is essential to examine both *instructional* and *institutional interactions*, for both constitute not only the full essence of schooling as cultural transmission but as the total formal educational experience of a student. Moreover, not only must we make school a less oppressive place, but we should seek as a society to improve the lives of children outside school as well. If we can do this, it will not be necessary to go through perverse machinations to save troubled schools under the pretense of charlatan-like scientific theories and their associated practices. Therefore, when we look at the arrangements made to accommodate today's so-called mildly handicapped student we are looking not at neutral or benevolent outcomes that research has provided, but instead, we are dealing with the institutionalization of sociological processes. The latter point has been the major concern of this work.

The implications of this radical socioeducational analysis are that we: (a) see better how American special education and LD have developed, (b) recognize more clearly the problematic course special education, especially of late via LD, has taken, and (c) are able to fomulate a more sensible future policy for educating the handicapped.

Future Practice And Policy

Many children are classified LD, and for that matter mild ED or MR, to draw funds from the federal government. Different funding methods must be promulgated for remedial programs to keep pupils with 'mild handicaps' out of the special education system (Sigmon, 1984 d). The expansion of special education as a result of the federal government's relatively recent massive involvement is an attempt to brace a public school system — primarily of late through the more palatable LD label and its associated programs — which reflects in many ways economic inequality and social problems of society as a whole. As a result, special education's true mission — to educate the moderately and severely handicapped — has been forgotten; and not only has it been made a scapegoat, but it has become subliminally politicized (Shapiro, 1980; Sigmon, 1985 b; Tomlinson, 1982).

Two highly essential points have emerged from the five university affiliated LD research institutes sponsored for four years by the federal government (through Title VI-G of PL91–230) which began operations in 1977 or 1978 (Kneedler and Hallahan, 1983). The work at the institute in Minnesota, which focused on LD classification decision making by school officials, reached the conclusion that it is very difficult to distinguish between children who actually may have mild LD and those who are simply underachievers (Epps, McGue and Ysseldyke, 1982; Ysseldyke, Algozzine, Shinn and McGue, 1982). The apolitical way of viewing this would be to acknowledge that there is an 'oversophistication' of the concept of LD (Algozzine and Ysseldyke, 1983). The other four LD research institutes, for the most part, developed sophisticated teaching methods which were highly effective with so-called LD students of all ages — they recognized that not all of the students they worked with were physiologically learning impaired. In essence, the four found that all LD students do learn, and such students learn but with careful and rigorous teaching methodology. The students they worked with were probably also motivated somewhat by the attention they received which facilitated their success.

It is the position of this author and probably that of most all the higher education-scholarly community, that the gains made by the research-educators on the study of dysfunctional learning styles (LD) — regardless of the LD genesis — and their concomitant advances in teaching techniques have not, by and large, been put into practice in the public schools. Furthermore, it is not believed here that a great many special educational programs for the LD employ the sophisticated techniques developed by the four LD research institutes, and many special educators at all levels are unaware of them. These techniques (which involve communication skills, the learning process, and academic strategies — as well as motivation) will not be described here because a discussion of teaching methodology is not the intent of this work (for this see Carnine, 1979; Kneedler and Hallahan, 1983). Rather, the purpose here is to articulate the problem which is that LD, an inherently good notion, is being abused and is used, for the most part, to gain monies to pay for educational tracks for those students who do not conform to the regular education programs — and who do not fit other special education labels. LD is a classification of and by default.

Policy and practice regarding LD should be changed, and as soon as possible. We must rapidly move away from the LD clinical classification to the newer LD 'practice model' to produce more effective teaching. Because of the progressive inclusion *ad nauseam* of more and more American schoolchildren into the ranks of the formally classified so-called mildly handicapped, 'The distinctions between remedial and special education are . . . increasingly arbitrary and difficult to make' (Kauffman, 1984, p. 5). The newer rigorous successful teaching techniques developed by the LD institutes and others should be employed with *all* students. Good students would be better, and so would the others. School districts should not have to classify students to get funding. The LD question is a societal problem, not an intrapsychic individual student problem. There would be fewer underachievers in society if less poverty existed in the cities and suburban schools were more humane. The LD clinical model now used serves only to stigmatize and segregate, inappropriately and unconscionably, most of the approximately $1\frac{3}{4}$-million American schoolchildren currently labeled LD.

The two following real anecdotes are quite telling. It quite recently was heard from a newly graduated urban high school student who was considered by local school officials to be 'only very mildly LD': 'I was in a special class. My grandmother thinks I was there because I'm retarded. That's not the reason. You see, I'm only brain damaged'. In the other situation, a third grade teacher in a suburban school requested a child study team evaluation of a student to determine eligibility for special education because the student was performing lower than expected, was occasionally not efficient with individual seat-work, and was not enthusiastic to work for a very authoritarian remedial reading teacher. This lone remedial teacher was the only option for extra help at this suburban school aside from special education. At the conference to interpret the child study team findings, the parent of this mid-third grader was told that 'weaknesses were a 2.8 grade level score on an individually administered reading test' and 'fidgety behavior during test sessions'. Also told was that: 'The neurologist did not find any real brain injury, but soft signs suggest the existence of a learning disability. So we would like to place your child in a special education resource room for two periods every day'. It is hoped that these sorts of experiences will become part of history, never to be repeated.

The basis for the scientific evidence for classifying what will soon be two million American students as LD is questionable and so are the tests used to identify such. There is, however, no doubt that many children do not learn very well or very much in most of today's regular classes. Some children may have LD caused by actual, severe neurological disorganization and would benefit from a special class. However, it is clear that the great majority of children classified LD have no internal problem. There are many students today in the public schools, labeled LD or not, who are resisters.

There is in operation a 'reproduction-resistance dialectic' between the schools and the conservative establishment-client it serves on the one hand, and the disenfranchised or disinterested student captives who are to be inculcated with certain values on the other. Educating children is but one of several functions of the schools. The field of LD must be viewed separately from school politics, and must adopt the newer practice model to educate students who have difficulty with school subjects rather than to become further co-opted as a means of segregating students who resist conventional schooling.

The special education tracks that have been created, LD and others, are really an attempt to conserve and perpetuate the culture and its institutions of which the school is an important one. And as inappropriate as these special education tracks are, especially those for the so-called mildly handicapped, they signify the ongoing social (class) and racial conflict. In this vein, Jones (1983) wrote a piece about socioeconomic retardation and schooling, and quoting from him: 'Low-income minority children constitute a disproportionately large share of students assigned to special education in public schools. Their . . . "problems" are, I would suggest, socially induced learning disabilities' (p. v). The rationale given today for labeling even the so-called mildly handicapped is that of individual biological defect. Earlier, specifically in the 1920s, entire groups in America — non-white or foreign born — were falsely often 'scientifically' shown to be defective. 'In a most interesting way, a study of biological determinism is a study in the sociology of science. For biological determinism not only categorizes individuals and groups but serves to legitimate extant social and political relations' (Selden, 1983, p. 177). Whereas the original, relatively small group of LD children probably did have some individual biological abnor-mality, i.e., brain damage, most all of the vast numbers classified LD now have absolutely no internal disorder of any kind whatsoever. This very smooth but rapid inclusion of the non-biologically disordered has become a camouflaged and actually a non-deliberate means of social control that has escaped until relatively recently a great deal of attention by even the most serious social critics.

> The selection of children for special education *appears* to be based on 'natural' inequalities so self-evident that even conflict-oriented sociologists have seldom questioned the naturalness, and the notion that certain children should naturally be categorised out of the normal educational system fitted in very well with a functionalist view of society. (Tomlinson, 1982, p. 68)

The current American special education structure — perhaps slightly designed for social control around 1900 — has become a significant accidental form of liberal institutional constraint for nonconformists; and cannot therefore be considered any sort of major covert conspiracy. The conservatives, however, seek a retrenchment of the expensive special educa-tion monolith which would entail unofficial tracking without labeling students in larger classes — special education class size is limited to small groups — in the public schools and/or the creation of private school incentives.

The US federal government has never really publicized a cogent or comprehensive policy — if one ever existed at all — regarding special education, or even, to some lesser extent, one about general education. In fact, education has only recently been elevated to an area of real, separate concern by the federal government when a Cabinet-level Department of Education was created by a somewhat liberal (Carter, Democratic Party) administration in the late 1970s. Because of this lack of policy two things have occurred. (a) Congress — as a result of various social pressures — has actually created a hodgepodge national special education policy which began in 1957 and culminated approximately twenty years later with Public Law 94–142 of 1975. And (b), as a result of this type of policy, some believe there is no policy at all, or policy is to 'a significant sense', created by 'street-level bureaucrats' at the school district level who 'are the policymakers' (Weatherley, 1979, p. 172). The school districts are the bottom line regard-ing implementation of policy, and this does produce cultural relativism in special education; but the districts ultimately operate according to state laws which comply with federal statutes and funding procedures.

Earlier discussed were the differences among various social philoso-phies, and to some extent, their educational implications. Special education policy, or lack of it, is dependent upon which of the major social philosophies is dominant. At this point in time in America, even though a conservative (Reagan, Republican Party) administration is in power and its corresponding reactionary political backlash is being felt, a national liberal special education policy is still in effect. Public Law 94–142 is a reflection of the prevailing liberal ideology, i.e., the gradual or piecemeal improvement of society and the egalitarian notion that all individuals — including the handicapped — have the right to an education. The conservative takes a more 'free market' position regarding education (see Imber and Namenson, 1983) in that students and their parents would fend for themselves in the marketplace of schools — with the concomitant belief that competition among schools would yield better quality education. Thus, during Ronald Reagan's first term in office, his administration attempted, without success, to reduce federal funding in support of education for the handicapped, modify or repeal PL94–142, do away with the Department of Education, and made fewer Americans eligible for college student loans. The conservatives want a reduced government role in the monetary support of schools, and do not necessarily see quality education for the masses as a right.

General education must not abdicate its role in educating low achieving or difficult children — even before we see a more humane transformation of society — by turning over responsibility of such students to special education. However, ordinary education would not have to do this if it were better supported fiscally and hopefully without reducing subsidies to the truly handicapped in the interim. Particularly regarding special education, not only should the handicapped be provided merely with a free and appropriate education, but it should be the best possible education. Much more should be done for the moderately and severely educationally handicapped. Those with the so-called mild handicaps are, by and large, really victims of a failing school system which mirrors a faulty, unequal politicoeconomic arrangement. Educational policies, for the handicapped or in general, involve us in the tension and arguments that exist between what is and what ought to be.

Summary

There are now over 4 $\frac{1}{4}$-million American schoolchildren formally involved in various types of special educational programs. Over half of these students are classified as having mild handicaps, the number is growing, and the rationales for these classifications are suspect. The major growth has been in the specific learning disabilities (LD) category which has increased since the

1976–77 schoolyear by 119 per cent to 1,745,871 pupils in 1982–83. The alarming increase of the so-called mildly handicapped student population, regardless of the label, may be the most serious ethical and practical dilemma facing American education today. The primary problem is that special education, through LD schooling tracks, has been perverted into a means of child control. The method for analyzing this problem is called radical socioeducational analysis (RSA), a new perspective which unlike the functional or empirical approaches, can offer fresh insights. RSA is basically qualitative as well as interpretive and explores the linkages between economic and cultural institutions. It is an interactive-interdisciplinary way of looking especially at the social conditions that impinge upon schooling arrangements and which in turn impact on social relationships. This is an open system based on Marx's historical dialectic conflict theory, plus the 'new' sociology of education which incorporates modern European sociopolitical theory and questions the ideological and epistemological foundations of conservative educational research. The scientific and conceptual bases for LD are weak. Some LD children have an individual medical defect as the term was originally conceived, but most are social victims who do not conform to regular education; and they are alleged, via inferential test data, to have dysfunctional internal psychological processing. Such youngsters are often school resisters who are merely uninterested and/or unmotivated. (Nevertheless, recent interactive educational research, typified by the recent LD institutes, has produced effective remedial learning techniques which can be applied to all students.) There is in effect a 'cultural reproduction-resistance dialectic' which portrays the pushes and pulls of social class struggle. This struggle has led to the inadvertent co-optation of special education by including millions of so-called mildly handicapped children instead of concentrating on the best possible education for the moderately and severely impaired.

Postscript: The Dialectic of Special Education

I do not believe any analysis, no matter how lengthy, is ever really complete or contains the last word on a topic; and this is especially true when dealing with subjects that are, for the most part, social constructions. Both special education and learning disabilities (LD) are such constructions of reality. Nevertheless, I believe this analysis was crafted in a manner which well explained the facts from a radical — and my personal — perspective. It is complete to my satisfaction. Yet, for those who believe this work is either incomplete or not radical enough, there are several items which naturally could and should be addressed — for those previously familiar or not with American special education's development, and regardless of their social philosophy.

After having learnt about my perspective on special education, the reaction by scholars (i.e., university professors) and school practitioners is almost always blatant hostility or outright praise. As far as I know, my work on special education, at this point in historical time, always elicits an emotional response from those close to the field. And because of this lack of neutrality, I consider my work a success — as I aimed at controversy to stimulate change in hard-held positions and practices. It is unsettling for many in special education to consider the questions I raise about the social purposes of the field and the nature of LD. But please keep in mind at stake are the lives and careers of children, which is why I examined the field so carefully. When I first began this project, I had a gut-feeling that most today in special education are wrongly schooled, but I am absolutely convinced of this now.

American special education research and practice tends not to be well informed by scholarship in history, sociology, or political economics. The narrow reliance on psychology and medicine for concepts, theories, and investigative models has limited scholarly development of this field, and probably has contributed to our current policy crises regarding identification of students as mildly handicapped (i.e., read mainly 'learning disabled'). The historical perspective is desperately lacking in special education. Through it I was able not only to weave in the effects of cultural and sociopolitical factors, but also to uncover some forgotten roots which affect current widespread thought and practice. Regarding the latter, perhaps the most important is the link from remedial education to the development of theories in learning disabilities. Moreover, the use of IQ tests to place children into special education tracks was shown not to be a recent phenomenon — many blacks as well as southern and eastern Europeans, who migrated to the northern United States in the early 20th century, had the dubious fate of being among the first. This is becoming more widely known. A radical analysis involves pointing out that tracking, under the guise of special education was: institutionalized early on a massive scale, had insidious effects on the futures of the individual students to the extent that they had their economic chances reduced, and only during relatively recent times has litigation against such practices been initiated. All too often special education writing too narrowly focuses on its own current research and becomes isolated — even from practices in other areas of education.

Perhaps not enough emphasis was given within the analysis of the role of a national statute entitled 'Public Law 94–142' (PL94–142), also called 'The Education for All Handicapped Children Act of 1975'. PL94–142 not only guaranteed educational rights, but civil rights as well. Having established by legislation that all handicapped had a right to free appropriate education, due process procedures, described in the Act, sought to provide a litigative potential in the event that states or local educational agencies continued to fail to provide equal access to education, and, more subtly, to provide parents and others with a quasi-judicial procedure to respond to such things as: (a) culture-fairness in testing, (b) multiple measures related to the suspected handicap, (c) a specific provision to avoid excessive reliance on a single professional group (a multidisciplinary evaluation), (d) least restrictive (educational) environment provisions, and (e) mainstreaming. The combined protections afforded via due process and through parent involvement and parent education, also required by law, were intended to insure that, to the extent possible, implementation of the Act would include informed consent of parents — if such can be legislated. A great humanitarian effort was expended by PL94–142's proponents — primarily parent and professional advocacy groups, such as the Council for Exceptional Children — in guiding its passage. Their intent was to first enfranchise the unserved and then the underserved exceptional child. The Act also mandates the federal government provide much of the funding for special education, and, unfortunately, this has been the engine driving most of today's so-called mildly handicapped into special programs. PL94–142 has become a very sharp and swift dual-edged sword.

The lack of clarity and purpose in the area of learning disabilities is extremely detrimental to the valid special education efforts with moderately to severely handicapped students. I cannot emphasize strongly enough the existence of mass confusion over the definition of LD, and this was why LD's roots were explored — and found to be in medicine. In any event, the proliferation of LD classes is unethical and a self-defeating activity.

I cannot stress more strongly that I do believe learning disabilities (LD) of neurological genesis exist. In my own school practice there have been a number of true LD students; i.e., those with obvious average intellect who have learning problems which were traced to some medical-related problem — prenatal illness; birth problem; postnatal disease, injury, illness; or a genetic disorder. The problem with the LD classification in particular is its inclusion of a multitude of underachievers without any contributing medical history.

One of my most important points in this book was to demonstrate a relationship between the student who is an educational resister and the usage of the special education apparatus. Whether the curriculum is unrelated to the learner's needs is less important than whether education responds to the uncooperative through punitive use of special education. The use of special programs for students labeled socially maladjusted and emotionally disturbed is the obvious response — I do not believe most of these two types are severely clinically pathological to warrant such labels or segregation. A more subtle punitive use of special placement is through the LD or mildly or educable mentally retarded (EMR) programs.

The regular education community runs the risk of becoming increasingly unwilling or unable to cope with those who are divergent from some average expectation for social and academic performance in schools. This latter item is critical to a radical analysis as it points the way to a major social dilemma in the not too distant future. Specifically, the day may come, left unchecked, when special education will be asked to serve all children below the fiftieth percentile! Obviously, ordinary education must develop accommodations in response to children with learning difficulties.

The history of inclusion and exclusion of atypical children in public schools and in private institutions has evolved steadily from gross assessments of physical, mental and emotional adequacies and inadequacies to a heavy reliance on procedures and evaluations — psychometric, psycholinguistic, perceptual as well as projective — designed to sort, rank and classify children for special education placement. The role of such inferential psychological test instruments has become imbedded in social, cultural and political forces which I challenge as invalid and indefensible in meeting the needs of children whose learning styles, abilities and aptitudes are different enough to require nontraditional teaching techniques and administrative accommodations. Despite my harsh criticism of current testing practice and my philosophic preference for no formal student testing but rather only educating, I know even in the most humane advanced societies — the latter may be a paradox — pupil evaluation of some sort is necessary to maintain order. Furthermore, aside from the anxiety it may cause, assessment need not be inherently nefarious — provided its use is well intentioned; i.e., to ensure quality education, and not merely to help control a youngster in the institution known as school. Both education and schooling are processes, but quite different types. Educating is to enable a student to develop thinking skills and, hopefully, useful facts. Schooling is, in the main, a custodial form of socialization among other lesser purposes. The point is assessment should be designed not merely for classification and placement purposes, but rather to determine what needs to be done to improve the learning of atypical children in an instructional setting. I agree with the intent of PL94–142 that all aspects of the child's cultural, ethnic, socioeconomic and linguistic environment need to be evaluated.

This work has been concerned more with form, educational arrangements and overall practices, as opposed to content, methods of instruction or theories of learning. Thus, in an overall way to bridge this gap, I maintain that assessment and intervention (instruction) should be integrally related. Moreover, the mildly handicapped should receive remedial instead of special education, or better yet, more attentive in-class (individualized) instruction. In this way we can move towards delimiting the LD, and other mildly handicapped, populations while serving those truly in need of special help in school. Having done this, special education can be directed away from serving society's need to control populations and towards maximizing everyone's potential and opportunity. I feel all of this was implicit throughout my radical analysis of special education; yet perhaps I am at fault for not being more explicit on these key topics within it. One final note along these lines: There are those who might be disappointed about my omission of instructional techniques; but as important as they are to any discussion on education, it was not my intention to include them as I was really more concerned over the larger area which is the sociology of special education.

Even though a serious situation exists with the over-representation of minority group members in American special education programs, I deliberately chose to do little direct analysis along this line for two reasons. First of all, there were several places wherein the actual US government figures were noted indicating how rather high the number of minorities is in special education. Moreover, and quite importantly, the relationship of minority concerns, especially those of blacks, to changes in special education was discussed. Secondly, because minority and recent immigrant status usually relegate people to lower socioeconomic status, I approached my topic, special education, from a *social class*, rather than a race/ethnic, perspective in keeping with a Marxian model. Thus, cultural bias is merely taken as a given against minorities — who are usually poor.

While there are some who find comfort in the fact that more minority students are now labeled LD rather than mildly or educable mentally retarded (EMR), I do not. Nor do I advocate labeling them anything at all — other than people with human needs — in order that their schools might receive the more readily available special education bounty. Schools with poor children, predominantly minority or not, should receive additional monies without first stigmatizing their students. This is why I wrote the book!

The very important concept of control requires some discussion to avoid confusion. I take the position whereby controlling simply is managing a student. It is a fact, attending an ordinary classroom requires a great deal of conformity to rules of decorum as well as achievement. At the same time, in most cases, the behavioral and academic standards for special classes/schools are lower. Inasmuch as compulsory attendance laws require students to attend school, special education makes it easier to manage those who do not or cannot conform. Control in this sense certainly does not mean making unreasonable demands or being removed from the system. On the contrary, control through special educational tracks keeps the nonconformist in the school system — and under supervision. The issue is, however, in this way, how much does the student benefit? Special education, then, becomes a convenient way for regular education teachers or administrators to get rid of youngsters who are difficult to teach or manage.

It has been written that good philosophy raises more questions than it answers. With this work, after having done a radical analysis of special education, one primary question comes to mind: Where do we go from here? This is obviously a situation in which a straightforward question necessitates a complex response. Yet, for the sake of parsimony, I should like to suggest that the solutions to special education's major problem, policy, reside outside education. School policy usually reflects conflicts in the larger society. Ergo, there is no doubt that the problem is more sociopolitical (systemic) than educational. The quest to educate the handicapped on the one hand and the mission of the schools to conserve culture regardless of the psychic costs to children on the other, ensures a perverted overall policy for special education.

References

ABRAMS, J.C. (1984) Interaction of neurological and emotional factors in learning disability. *Learning Disabilities*, **3**, 27–37.

ALGOZZINE, R.F. (1976) Attractiveness as a biasing factor in teacher-pupil interactions (Doctoral dissertation, Pennsylvania State University, 1975). *Dissertation Abstracts International*, **36**, 7059A.

ALGOZZINE, R. and ABRAMS, J. (1984, April) Learning disabilities: Professional dilemma or diagnostic scandal? Symposium conducted at the 16th Annual Convention of the National Association of School Psychologists, Philadelphia. (Listed in *Convention '84* pamphlet, p. 2).

ALGOZZINE, R.F. and SUTHERLAND, J. (1977) Non-psychoeducational foundations of learning disabilities. *Journal of Special Education*, **11**, 91–98.

ALGOZZINE, B. and YSSELDYKE, J. (1983) Learning disabilities as a subset of school failure: The oversophistication of a concept. *Exceptional Children*, **50**, 242–246.

ALGOZZINE, B., YSSELDYKE, J.E. and CHRISTENSEN, S. (1983) An analysis of the incidence of special class placement: The masses are burgeoning. *Journal of Special Education*, **17**, 141–147.

AMERICAN PSYCHIATRIC ASSOCIATION. (1980) *Diagnostic and statistical manual of mental disorders* (3rd ed.). Washington, DC: Author.

APPLE, M.W. (1979) *Ideology and curriculum*. Boston and London: Routledge and Kegan Paul.

ARTER, J.A. and JENKINS, J.R. (1977) Examining the benefits and prevalence of modality considerations in special education. *Journal of Special Education*, **11**, 281–298.

ARTER, J.A. and JENKINS, J.R. (1979) Differential diagnosis-prescriptive teaching: A critical appraisal. *Review of Educational Research*, **49**, 517–555.

BANNATYNE, A. (1971) *Language, reading and learning disabilities*. Springfield, IL: Thomas.

BARSCH, R.H. (1963, November 24) *Motor learning: A spatial phenomenon*. Speech delivered at the Annual Convention of the American Academy of Cerebral Palsy.

BARSCH, R.H. (1966) *The movigenic curriculum* (Bulletin No. 25). Madison, WI: Bureau for Handicapped Children, State Department of Public Instruction.

BARSCH, R.H. (1967) *Achieving perceptual motor efficiency: A space-oriented approach to learning*. Seattle, WA: Special Child Publications.

BARSCH, R.H. (1968) Perspectives on learning disabilities: The vectors of a new convergence. *Journal of Learning Disabilities*, **1**, 4–20.

BASTIAN, H.C. (1887) On different kinds of aphasia, with special reference to their classification and ultimate pathology. *British Medical Journal* (Vol. 2), 931–936; Pt. 2, 985–990.

BECKER, W.C. (Ed.). (1971) *An empirical basis for change in education: Selections on behavioral psychology for teachers*. Chicago: Science Research Associates.

BECKER, W.C. and CARNINE, D.W. (1982) Direct instruction: A behavior theory model for comprehensive educational intervention with the disadvantaged. In S.W. BIJOU and R. RUIZ (Eds.), *Behavior modification: Contributions to education* (pp. 145–210). Hillsdale, NJ: Lawrence Erlbaum Associates.

BEERY, K.E. (1972) *Models for mainstreaming*. Sioux Falls, SD: Adapt Press.

BENDER, L. (1938) *A visual motor gestalt test and its clinical use* (Research Monographs No. 3). New York: American Orthopsychiatric Association.

BENTON, A.L. (1945) A visual retention test for clinical use. *Archives of Neurology and Psychiatry*, **54**, 212–216.

BENYON, S.D. (1968) *Intensive programming for slow learners*. Columbus, OH: Merrill.

BERNSTEIN, B. (1975) *Class, codes and control. Vol. 3: Towards a theory of educational transmissions*. London: Routledge and Kegan Paul.

BLATT, B. (1960) Some persistently recurring assumptions concerning the mentally subnormal. *Training School Bulletin*, **57**, 48–59.

BLATT, B. (1982) On the heels of psychology. *Journal of Learning Disabilities*, **15**, 52–53.

BOUILLAUD, J. (1825) Recherches cliniques propres à démontrer que la perte de la parole correspond à la lésion des lobules antérieurs du cerveau. *Archives Général de Medical*, **8**, 25–45.

BOURDIEU, P. and PASSERON, J.-C. (1977) *Reproduction in education, society and culture* (R. NICE, Trans.). London and Beverly Hills, CA: Sage. (Original work published 1970).

BOWLES, S. and GINTIS, H. (1976) *Schooling in capitalist America: Educational reform and the contradictions of economic life*. New York: Basic Books.

BRADY, P.M., MANNI, J.L. and WINIKUR, D.W. (1983) A three-tiered model for the assessment of culturally and linguistically different children. *Psychology in the Schools*, **20**, 52–58.

BRANN, E.T. (1979) *Paradoxes of education in a republic*. Chicago: University of Chicago Press.

BROCA, P. (1861 a) Remarques sur le siège de la faculté du langage articulé, suives d'une observation d'aphémie. *Bulletin de la Société d'Anatomie de Paris*, **6**, 330–357.

BROCA, P. (1861 b) Nouvelle observation d'aphémie produite par une lésion de la mortié posterieure de deuxième et troisième circonvolutions frontales. *Bulletin de la Société d'Anatomie de Paris*, **6**, 398–407.

BRYAN, T., PEARL, R., DONAHUE, M., BRYAN, J. and PFLAUM, S. (1983) The Chicago Institute for the study of learning disabilities. *Exceptional Education Quarterly*, **4**, 1–22.

BUCK-MORSS, S. (1975) Socioeconomic bias in Piaget's theory and its implications for cross-culture studies. *Human Development*, **18**, 35–49.

BUSS, A.R. (1979) *A dialectical psychology*. New York: Irvington Publishers.

CARNINE, D. (1979) Direct instruction: A successful system for educationally high-risk children. *Journal of Curriculum Studies*, **7**, 29–45.

CAWLEY, J.F., GOODSTEIN, H.A. and BURROW, W.H. (1972) *The slow learner and the reading problem*. Springfield, IL: Thomas.

CHAVES, I.M. (1977) Historical overview of special education in the United States. In P. BATES, T.L. WEST and R.B. SCHMERL (Eds), *Mainstreaming: Problems, potentials, and perspectives* (pp. 25–41). Minneapolis, MN: National Support Systems Project.

CLEMENTS, S.D. and PETERS, J.E. (1962) Minimal brain dysfunctions in the school-age child: Diagnosis and treatment. *Archives of General Psychiatry*, **6**, 185–197.

CLEUGH, M.F. (1957) *The slow learner: Some educational principles and policies*. London: Methuen.

COLES, G.S. (1978) The learning-disabilities test battery: Empirical and social issues. *Harvard Educational Review*, **48**, 313–340.

COLES, G.S. (1983) The use of Soviet psychological theory in understanding learning dysfunctions. *American Journal of Orthopsychiatry*, **53**, 619–628.

COLLINS, R. and CAMBLIN, L.D., Jr. (1983) The politics and science of learning disability classification: Implications for black children. *Contemporary Education*, **54**, 113–118.

COMPTROLLER GENERAL OF THE UNITED STATES. (1981, September 30) *Disparities still exist in who gets special education* (IPE-81-1; Report to the chairman, subcommittee on select education, committee on education and labor, House of Representatives). Washington, DC: U.S. General Accounting Office.

CONNOR, F.P. (1983) Improving school instruction for learning disabled children: The Teachers College Institute. *Exceptional Education Quarterly*, **4**, 23–44.

CREMIN, L.A. (1961) *The transformation of the school: Progressivism in American education, 1876–1957*. New York: Knopf.

CRUICKSHANK, W.M. (1967) The development of education for exceptional children. In W.M. CRUICKSHANK and G.O. JOHNSON (Eds), *Education of exceptional children and youth* (2nd ed., pp. 3–42). Englewood Cliffs, NJ: Prentice-Hall.

CRUICKSHANK, W.M. (1976) William M. Cruickshank. In J.M. KAUFFMAN and D.P. HALLAHAN (Eds), *Teaching children with learning disabilities: Personal perspectives* (pp. 94–127). Columbus, OH: Merrill.

CRUICKSHANK, W.M. (1983) Straight is the bamboo tree. *Journal of Learning Disabilities*, **16**, 191–197.

CRUICKSHANK, W.M., BENTZEN, F.A., RATZEBURG, F.H. and TANNHAUSER, T. (1961) *A teaching method for brain-injured and hyperactive children*. Syracuse, NY: Syracuse University Press.

CRUICKSHANK, W.M. and HALLAHAN, D.P. (1973) Alfred A. Strauss: Pioneer in learning disabilities. *Exceptional Children*, **39**, 321–327.

CRUICKSHANK, W.M. and JOHNSON, G.O. (Eds). (1967) *Education of exceptional children and youth* (2nd ed.). Englewood Cliffs, NJ: Prentice-Hall.

CURTI, M.E. (1959) *The social ideas of American educators* (rev. ed.). Paterson, NJ: Pageant Books.

CURTIS, B. (1984) Capitalist development and educational reform: Comparative material from England, Ireland and Upper Canada to 1850. *Theory and Society*, **13**, 41–68.

DAMICO, A.J. (1978) *Individuality and community: The social and political thought of John*

Dewey. Gainesville: University Presses of Florida.

D'ANGELO, E. (1982) Education and revolutionary change. *Revolutionary World*, **49–50**, 135–145.

DAVIS, W.E. (1980) *Educator's resource guide to special education: Terms, laws, tests, and organizations*. Boston: Allyn and Bacon.

DAWE, A. (1970) The two sociologies. *British Journal of Sociology*, **21**, 207–218.

DELACATO, C.H. (1959) *The treatment and prevention of reading problems: The neuropsychological approach*. Springfield, IL: Thomas.

DENO, E. (1970) Special education as developmental capital. *Exceptional Children*, **37**, 229–237.

DESHLER, D.D. (1978) New research institutes for the study of learning disabilities. *Learning Disability Quarterly*, **1**, 68.

DEWEY, J. (1981) From absolutism to experimentalism. In J.J. MCDERMOTT (Ed.), *The philosophy of John Dewey. Two volumes in one* (pp. 1–13). Chicago: University of Chicago Press. (Original work published 1930).

DIVOKY, D. (1974) Education's latest victim: The 'LD' kid. *Learning*, **3**, 20–25.

DOLPHIN, J.E. (1950) *A study of certain aspects of the psychopathology of cerebral palsy children*. Unpublished doctoral dissertation, Syracuse University.

DUNN, L.M. (1968) Special education for the mildly retarded — Is much of it justifiable? *Exceptional Children*, **35**, 5–22.

DUNN, L.M. (1973) An overview. In L.M. DUNN (Ed.), *Exceptional children in the schools: Special education in transition* (2nd ed., pp. 1–62). New York: Holt, Rinehart and Winston.

Education of handicapped children: Implementation of part B of the handicapped act. (1977, August 23) *Federal Register*, **42**, 42474–42518.

EISENSON, J. (1954) *Examining for aphasia: A manual for the examination of aphasia and related disturbances*. New York: The Psychological Corporation.

ELLIOTT, C.D. (1983) *British ability scales, manual 1: Introductory handbook*. Windsor, Berks, England: NFER-Nelson.

ELLIS, J.W. (1973) *The slow to learn*. London: Priority Press.

ENGLEMANN, S. (1969) *Preventing failure in the primary grades*. Chicago: Science Research Associates.

ENGLEMANN, S. and CARNINE, D. (1969) *Distar arithmetic: An instructional system*. Chicago: Science Research Associates.

EPPS, S., MCGUE, M. and YSSELDYKE, J.E. (1982) Interjudge agreement in classifying students as learning disabled. *Psychology in the Schools*, **19**, 209–220.

FARNHAM-DIGGORY, S. (1978) *Learning disabilities: A psychological approach*. Cambridge, MA: Harvard University Press.

FARRELL, G. (1956) *The story of blindness*. Cambridge, MA: Harvard University Press.

FERNALD, G. (1943) *Remedial techniques in basic school subjects*. New York: McGraw-Hill.

FERNALD, G. and KELLER, H. (1921) The effect of kinesthetic factors in the development of word recognition in the case of nonreaders. *Journal of Educational Research*, **4**, 355–377.

FILLER, J.W., Jr., ROBINSON, C.C., SMITH, R.A., VINCENT-SMITH, L.J., BRICKER, D.D. and BRICKER, W.A. (1975) Mental retardation. In N. HOBBS (Ed.), *Issues in the classification of children, Vol. I: A sourcebook on categories, labels, and their consequences* (pp. 194–238). San Francisco: Jossey-Bass.

Fisk, J.L. and Rourke, B.P. (1983) Neuropsychological subtyping of learning-disabled children: History, methods, implications. *Journal of Learning Disabilities*, **16**, 529–531.

Foster, S.G. (1984, April 25) Rise in learning-disabled pupils fuels concern in states, districts. *Education Week*, pp. 1, 18.

Freire, P. (1970) *Pedagogy of the oppressed* (M.B. Ramos, Trans.). New York: Herder and Herder.

Frostig, M., Lefever, D.W. and Whittlesey, R.B. (1961) A developmental test of visual perception for evaluating normal and neurologically handicapped children. *Perceptual and Motor Skills*, **12**, 383–394.

Gaddis, E.A. (1971) *Teaching the slow learner in the regular classroom*. Belmont, CA: Fearon-Pitman.

Gall, F.J. (1807) *Craniologie ou découvertes nouvelles concernant le cerveau, le crâne et les organes*. Paris: Necelle.

Gardner, E.M. (1984, May 11) The education crisis: Washington shares the blame (No. 351). *The Heritage Foundation Backgrounder*.

Geschwind, N. (1962) The anatomy of acquired disorders of reading. In J. Money (Ed.), *Reading disability: Progress and research needs in dyslexia* (pp. 115–128). Baltimore, MD: Johns Hopkins Press.

Getman, G.N. (1962) *The school skill tracing board*. Minneapolis, MN: Programs to Accelerate School Success (PASS).

Giarelli, J.M. (1982) [Review of *Progressive education: A Marxist interpretation*]. *Educational Studies*, **13**, 464–471.

Gibson, J.T. (1984) Comparative views on educating students with special needs: American and Soviet approaches. *School Psychology International*, **5**, 91–96.

Gill, G.R. (1980) *Meanness mania: The changed mood*. Washington, DC: Howard University Press.

Gillingham, A. and Stillman, B.W. (1936) *Remedial work for reading, spelling, and penmanship*. New York: Sachett and Wilhelms.

Gilmore, M.I. (1956) A comparison of selected legislative provisions for special education in local districts in Illinois with those of other states. *Exceptional Children*, **22**, 237–248.

Giroux, H.A. (1980) [Review of *Antonio Gramsci: Conservative schooling for radical politics*]. *Telos*, **45**, 215–225.

Giroux, H.A. (1981) *Ideology culture and the process of schooling*. Philadelphia: Temple University Press.

Giroux, H.A. (1983) *Theory and resistance in education: A pedagogy for the opposition*. South Hadley, MA: Bergin and Garvey.

Goldstein, H., Moss, J.W. and Jordan, L.J. (1965) *The efficacy of special class training on the development of mentally retarded children*. Urbana: University of Illinois Institute for Research on Exceptional Children.

Goldstein, K. (1942) *Aftereffects of brain injuries in war*. New York: Grune and Stratton.

Gramsci, A. (1971) *Selections from the prison notebooks* (Q. Hoare and G. Smith, Eds and Trans.). New York: International. (Original work published 1941).

Gross, B. and Gross, R. (Eds.). (1969) *Radical school reform*. New York: Simon and Schuster.

Guskin, A.E. and Guskin, S.L. (1970) *A social psychology of education*. Reading, MA: Addison-Wesley.

HAIGH, G. (1977) *Teaching slow learners*. London: Temple Smith.

HALL, G.S. (1883) The contents of children's minds. *The Princeton Forum*, **11**, 249–272.

HALL, G.S. (1900) Child-study and its relation to education. *The Forum*, **29**, 688–702.

HALL, G.S. (1901–2) The ideal school as based on child study. *The Forum*, **32**, 24–39.

HALLAHAN, D.P. and CRUICKSHANK, W.M. (1973) *Psychoeducational foundations of learning disabilities*. Englewood Cliffs, NJ: Prentice-Hall.

HALLAHAN, D.P. and KAUFFMAN, J.M. (1976) *Introduction to learning disabilities: A psycho-behavioral approach*. Englewood Cliffs, NJ: Prentice-Hall.

HALLGREN, B. (1950–51) Specific dyslexia (congenital word-blindness): A clinical and genetic study. *Acta Psychiatrica et Neurologica Scandinavica*, **65** (Suppl. 65), 1–287.

HARAP, H. (1936) Differentiation of curriculum practices and instruction in elementary schools. *The grouping of pupils: Thirty-fifth yearbook, Pt. 1, National Society for the Study of Education*, 161–172.

HARRIS, K. (1979) *Education and knowledge: The structured misrepresentation of reality*. London: Routledge and Kegan Paul.

HATHAWAY, W. (1966) *Education and health of the partially seeing child* (4th ed., by F.M. FOOTE, D. BRYAN and H. GIBBONS). New York: Columbia University Press.

HEAD, H. (1926) *Aphasia and kindred disorders of speech* (Vol. I and II). London: Cambridge University Press.

HECK, A.O. (1940) *The education of exceptional children; its challenge to teachers, parents, and laymen*. New York: McGraw-Hill.

HEDMAN, C.G. (1979) The "deschooling" controversy revisited: A defense of Illich's 'participatory socialism'. *Educational Theory*, **29**, 109–116.

HEGGE, T.G., KIRK, S.A. and KIRK, W.D. (1936) *Remedial reading drills*. Ann Arbor, MI: George Wahr.

HERMAN, K. (1959) *Reading disability*. Springfield, IL: Thomas.

HEWETT, F.M. (1974) *Education of exceptional learners*. Boston: Allyn and Bacon.

HINSHELWOOD, J. (1917) *Congenital word blindness*. London: Lewis.

HOBBS, N. (1975) *The futures of children: Categories, labels, and their consequences*. San Francisco, CA: Jossey-Bass.

HOELTKE, G.M. (1966) Effectiveness of special class placement for educable mentally retarded children (Doctoral dissertation, University of Nebraska, 1966). *Dissertation Abstracts*, **27**, 3311A.

HOFFMAN, E. (1974) The treatment of deviance by the educational system: History. In W.C. RHODES and S. HEAD (Eds), *A study of child variance, Vol. III: Service delivery systems* (pp. 41–79). Franklin, TN: New Academic Village.

HOWE, S.G. (1858) *Third and final report on the Experimental School for Teaching and Training Idiotic Children and the first report of the trustees of the Massachusetts School for Idiotic and Feebleminded Youth, 1852–1858* (House Document No. 57). Cambridge: Commonwealth of MA.

HURN, C.J. (1978) *The limits and possibilities of schooling: An introduction to the sociology of education*. Boston: Allyn and Bacon.

ILLICH, I. (1970) *Deschooling society*. New York: Harper and Row.

IMBER, M. and NAMENSON, J. (1983) Is there a right to education in America? *Educational Theory*, **33**, 97–111.

INGRAM, C.P. (1960) *The education of the slow-learning child* (3rd ed.). New York: Ronald. (Original work published 1935, second edition 1953).

JACKSON, J.H. (1874) On the nature and duality of the brain. *Medical Press and Circular*, **1**, 19, 41, 63.

JOHNSON, G.O. (1962) Special education for the mentally handicapped — A paradox. *Exceptional Children*, **29**, 62–69.

JOHNSON, G.O. (1963) *Education for the slow learners*. Englewood Cliffs, NJ: Prentice-Hall.

JOHNSON, G.O. and MYKLEBUST, H.R. (1967) *Learning disabilities: Educational principles and practices*. New York: Grune and Stratton.

JOHNSON, J.L. (1969) Special education and the inner city: A challenge for the future or another means for cooling the mark out? *Journal of Special Education*, **3**, 241–251.

JONES, P.E. (1983) Special education and socioeconomic retardation. *Journal for Special Educators*, **19**(4), v–ix.

KALUGER, G. and KOLSON, C.J. (1969) *Reading and learning disabilities*. Columbus, OH: Merrill.

KARLIN, M.S. and BERGER, R. (1969) *Successful methods for teaching the slow learner*. West Nyack, NY: Parker.

KASS, C.E. and MYKLEBUST, H.R. (1969) Learning disability: An educational definition. *Journal of Learning Disabilities*, **2**, 38–40.

KAUFFMAN, J.M. (1984) From the senior editor. *Remedial and Special Education*, **5**(1), 5.

KELLY, E.J. (1971) *Philosophical perspectives in special education*. Columbus, OH: Merrill.

KEPHART, N.C. (1971) *The slow learner in the classroom* (2nd ed.). Columbus, OH: Merrill. (1st ed. published 1960).

KERR, J. (1897) School hygiene in its mental, moral and physical aspects. *Royal Statistical Society Journal*, **60**, 613–680.

KIRK, S.A. (1962) *Educating exceptional children*. Boston: Houghton Mifflin. (The second edition was published in 1972).

KIRK, S.A. (1963) Behavioral diagnosis and remediation of learning disabilities. *Proceedings of the first annual meeting of the ACLD conference on exploration into the problems of the perceptually handicapped child*, **1**, 1–7. (Paper presented April 6).

KIRK, S.A. (1966) *The diagnosis and remediation of psycholinguistic disabilities*. Urbana: University of Illinois Press.

KIRK, S.A. (1976) Samual A. Kirk. In J.M. KAUFFMAN and D.P. HALLAHAN (Eds), *Teaching children with learning disabilities: Personal perspectives* (pp. 238–269). Columbus, OH: Merrill.

KIRK, S.A. and BATEMAN, B. (1962) Diagnosis and remediation of learning disabilities. *Exceptional Children*, **29**, 73–78.

KIRK, S.A. and GALLAGHER, J.J. (1979) *Educating exceptional children* (3rd ed.). Boston: Houghton Mifflin. (Original work published 1962).

KIRK, S.A. and McCARTHY, J.J. (1961) The Illinois test of psycholinguistic abilities — an approach to differential diagnosis. *American Journal of Mental Deficiency*, **66**, 399–412.

KIRK, S.A., McCARTHY, J.J. and KIRK, W.D. (1968) *Illinois test of psycholinguistic abilities* (rev. ed.). Urbana: University of Illinois Press.

KIRK, S.A. and McCARTHY, J.M. (Eds.). (1975) *Learning disabilities: Selected ACLD papers*. Boston: Houghton Mifflin.

KNEEDLER, R.D. and HALLAHAN, D.P. (Eds.). (1983) Research in learning disabilities: Summaries of the institutes [Special issue]. *Exceptional Education Quarterly*, **4**(1).

KOCH appoints 11 to study special education. (1984, April 29) *The New York Times*, p. 47.

KOPPITZ, E.M. (1963) *The Bender gestalt test for young children.* New York: Grune and Stratton.

KUSSMAUL, A. (1877) *Die störungen der sprache.* Leipzig: F.C.W. Vogel.

L'ABATE, L. and CURTIS, L.T. (1975) *Teaching the exceptional child.* Philadelphia: Saunders.

LARRY P. v. RILES (1979) C–71–2270, 343 F. Supp. 1306 (N.D. Cal. 1972); Aff'd. 502 F. 2d 963 (9th Cir. 1974); 495 F. Supp. 926 (N.D. Cal. 1979).

LERNER, J.W. (1971) *Children with learning disabilities: Theories, diagnosis, and teaching strategies.* Boston: Houghton Mifflin.

LEVITAS, M. (1974) *Marxist perspectives in the sociology of education.* London: Routledge and Kegan Paul.

LOEB, V. (1984, April 25) Philadelphia to study classification of learning-disabled pupils: Superintendent finds rise in number 'questionable'. *Education Week*, pp. 1, 15.

LUCAS, C.J. (1972) *Our Western educational heritage.* New York: Macmillan.

MANN, L. (1971 a) Perceptual training revisited: The training of nothing at all. *Rehabilitation Literature*, **32**, 322–327, 335.

MANN, L. (1971 b) Psychometric phrenology and the new faculty psychology: The case against ability assessment and training. *Journal of Special Education*, **5**, 3–14.

MANN, L. (1979) *On the trail of process: A historical perspective on cognitive processes and their training.* New York: Grune and Stratton.

MANN, L., CARTWRIGHT, G.P., KENOWITZ, L.A., BOYER, C.W., Jr., METZ, C.M. and WOLFORD, B. (1984) The child service demonstration centers: A summary report. *Exceptional Children*, **50**, 532–540.

MANN, L., DAVIS, C.H., BOYER, C.W., Jr., METZ, C.M. and WOLFORD, B. (1983) LD or not LD, that was the question: A retrospective analysis of child service demonstration centers' compliance with the federal definition of learning disabilities. *Journal of Learning Disabilities*, **16**, 14–17.

MANNI, J.L., WINIKUR, D.W. and KELLER, M. (1980) *The status of minority group representation in special education programs in New Jersey: A summary report.* Trenton: NJ State Department of Education.

MARIE, P. (1906) Revision de la question de l'aphasie: La troisième circonvolution frontale gauche ne joue aucum rôle spéciale dans la fonction du langage. *Sermaine Médicale*, **26**, 241–247.

MARTINSON, B. and STRAUSS, A.A. (1940) Education and treatment of an imbecile boy of the exogenous type. *American Journal of Mental Deficiency*, **45**, 274–280.

MARX, K. (1941) Theses on Feuerbach. In F. ENGELS, *Ludwig Feuerbach and the outcome of classical German philosophy* (pp. 82–84). New York: International. (Work written in 1845).

McCARTHY, J.J. and KIRK, S.A. (1961) *The Illinois test of psycholinguistic abilities, experimental edition, examiner's manual.* Urbana: University of Illinois Press.

McCARTHY, J.J. and McCARTHY, J.F. (1969) *Learning disabilities.* Boston: Allyn and Bacon.

McGINNIS, M.A., KLEFFNER, F.R. and GOLDSTEIN, P. (1956) Teaching aphasic children. *Volta Review*, **58**, 239–244.

McKNIGHT, R.T. (1982) The learning disability myth in American education. *Journal of Education*, **164**, 351–359.

MONROE, M. (1928) Methods for diagnosis and treatment of cases of reading disabilities. *Genetic Psychology Monographs*, **4**, 355–456.

MONROE, M. (1932) *Children who cannot read*. Chicago: University of Chicago Press.

MORGAN, W.P. (1896) A case of congenital word blindness. *British Medical Journal* (Vol. 2), 1378.

MYERS, P.I. and HAMMILL, D.D. (1969) *Methods for learning disorders*. New York: Wiley.

MYERS, P.I. and HAMMILL, D.D. (1982) *Learning disabilities: Basic concepts, assessment practices, and instructional strategies*. Austin, TX: Pro-Ed.

MYKLEBUST, H. (1955) Training aphasic children. *Volta Review*, **57**, 149–157.

NAHEM, J. (1981) *Psychology and psychiatry today: A Marxist view*. New York: International.

NATIONAL ADVISORY COMMITTEE ON HANDICAPPED CHILDREN. (1968) *First annual report, subcommittee on education of the committee on labor and public welfare, U.S. Senate*. Washington, DC: U.S. Government Printing Office.

NEILL, A.S. (1960) *Summerhill: A radical approach to child rearing*. New York: Hart.

NELSON, C.C. and SCHMIDT, L.J. (1970) The question of the efficacy of special class. *Exceptional Children*, **37**, 381–384.

NEW JERSEY COMMISSIONER OF EDUCATION'S COMMISSION ON THE EDUCATION OF THE HANDICAPPED. (1965) *The education of handicapped children in New Jersey 1954–1964*. Trenton: NJ State Department of Education.

NEW JERSEY DEPARTMENT OF EDUCATION. (1980, September). *Guidelines for the evaluation of culturally and linguistically different children for purposes of educable mentally retarded classification*. Trenton, NJ: Author.

ORTON, S.T. (1925) Word blindness in school children. *Archives of Neurology and Psychiatry*, **14**, 581–615.

ORTON, S.T. (1928) Specific reading disability — Strephosymbolia. *Journal of the American Medical Association*, **90**, 1095–1099.

ORTON, S.T. (1937) *Reading, writing and speech problems in children*. New York: Norton.

OSGOOD, C.E. (1953) *Method and theory in experimental psychology*. New York: Oxford University Press.

POSTMAN, N. and WEINGARTNER, C. (1969) *Teaching as a subversive activity*. New York: Delacorte.

PRITCHARD, D.G. (1963) *Education and the handicapped: 1760–1960*. London: Routledge and Kegan Paul.

RADFORD-HILL, S. (1984) *Perspectives on school psychology and advocacy: Preliminary report of the NASP/NCAS task force on school psychology and advocacy*. Unpublished manuscript. (Chicago: Designs for Change).

REAGAN, T. (1980) The foundations of Ivan Illich's social thought. *Educational Theory*, **30**, 293–306.

REYNOLDS, M.C. (1962) A framework for considering some issues in special education. *Exceptional Children*, **28**, 367–370.

REYNOLDS, M.C. (1975) Trends in special education: Implications for measurement. In M.C. REYNOLDS and W. HIVELY (Eds), *Domain-referenced testing in special education* (pp. 15–28). Minneapolis: University of MN Leadership Training Institute/Special Education.

RIEGEL, K.F. (1979) *Foundations of dialectical psychology.* New York: Academic Press.

RIPPA, S.A. (1980) *Education in a free society: An American history* (4th ed.). New York: Longman.

ROBINSON, H.B. and ROBINSON, N.M. (1965) *The mentally retarded child: A psychological approach.* New York: McGraw-Hill.

ROSENTHAL, R. and JACOBSON, L. (1968) *Pygmalion in the classroom.* New York: Holt, Rinehart and Winston.

ROSS, A.O. (1977) *Learning disability: The unrealized potential.* New York: McGraw-Hill.

ROUSSEAU, J.J. (1974) *Emile.* London: J.B. Dent

RUBIN, E.Z., SIMSON, C.B. and BETWEE, M.C. (1966) *Emotionally handicapped children and the elementary school.* Detroit: Wayne State University Press.

RUSSELL, W.L. (1941) A psychopathic department of an American general hospital in 1908. *American Journal of Psychiatry,* **98**, 229–237.

SARASON, S.B. (1949) *Psychological problems in mental deficiency.* New York: Harper.

SARUP, M. (1978) *Marxism and education: A study of phenomenological and Marxist approaches to education.* London: Routledge and Kegan Paul.

SCHMID, R.E. (1979) Historical perspective. In C.D. MERCER (Ed.), *Children and adolescents with learning disabilities* (pp. 3–36). Columbus, OH: Merrill.

SCHRAG, P. and DIVOKY, D. (1975) *The myth of the hyperactive child: And other means of child control.* New York: Pantheon.

SCHUELL, H., JENKINS, J.J. and JIMENEZ-PABON, E. (1964) *Aphasia in adults.* New York: Haeber Medical Division, Harper.

SCHUMAKER, J.B. and DESHLER, D.D. (1983, May) *Setting demand variables: A major factor in program planning for the LD adolescent.* Unpublished manuscript, University of Kansas, Institute for Research in Learning Disabilities.

SEDLAK, R.A. and WEENER, P. (1973) Review of research on the Illinois test of psycholinguistic abilities. In L. MANN and D.A. SABATINO (Eds), *The first review of special education* (pp. 113–163). Philadelphia: JSE Press.

SELDEN, S. (1983) Biological determinism and the ideological roots of student classification. *Journal of Education,* **165**, 175–191.

SENF, G.M. (1981) Issues surrounding the diagnosis of learning disabilities: Child handicap versus failure of the child-school interaction. In T.R. KRATOCHWILL (Ed.), *Advances in school psychology* (Vol. I, pp. 83–131). Hillsdale, NJ: Lawrence Erlbaum Associates.

SHAPIRO, H.S. (1980) Society, ideology and the reform of special education: A study in the limits of educational change. *Educational Theory,* **30**, 211–223.

SHARP, R. (1980) *Knowledge, ideology and the politics of schooling: Towards a Marxist analysis of education.* London: Routledge and Kegan Paul.

SHELTON, B.O. (1971) *Teaching and guiding the slow learner.* West Nyack, NY: Parker.

SIEGEL, L.S. and RYAN, E.B. (1984) Reading disability as language disorder. *Remedial and Special Education,* **5**(3), 28–33.

SIEVERS, D.J. (1956) Development and standardization of a test of psycholinguistic growth in preschool children (Doctoral dissertation, University of Illinois, 1955). *Dissertation Abstracts,* **16**, 286–287.

SIGMON, S.B. (1983 a) The history and future of educational segregation. *Journal for*

Special Educators, **19**(4), 1–15.

SIGMON, S.B. (1983 b) Performance of American schoolchildren on Raven's colored progressive matrices scale. *Perceptual and Motor Skills*, **56**, 484–486.

SIGMON, S.B. (1984 a) Interactionistic psychology: A fourth force? *Psychological Reports*, **54**, 156.

SIGMON, S.B. (1984 b) Interactionism: Force four psychology. *Professional Psychology: Research and Practice*, **15**, 470–471.

SIGMON, S.B. (1984 c) Notes on a relationship between Piagetian childhood thought development and Raven's colored progressive matrices. *Perceptual and Motor Skills*, **58**, 436–438.

SIGMON, S.B. (1984 d) Comments on the so-called learning disability myth in American education. *Reading Improvement*, **21**, 103–104.

SIGMON, S.B. (1985 a) *Radical socioeducational analysis*. New York: Irvington Publishers.

SIGMON, S.B. (1985 b) ['Over the last few years . . . learning disabilities. . . .' Letter to the editor]. *Remedial and Special Education*, **6**(1), 5–6.

SKINNER, B.F. (1965) The technology of teaching. *Proceedings of the Royal Society*, **162B**, 427–443. (Speech delivered November 19, 1964).

SMITH, H.W. and KENNEDY, W.A. (1967) Effects of three educational programs on mentally retarded children. *Perceptual and Motor Skills*, **24**, 174.

SMITH, N.B. (1961) What have we accomplished in reading? — A review of the past fifty years. *Elementary English*, **38**, 141–150.

SPALDING, R.B. and SPALDING, W.T. (1962) *The writing road to reading, a modern method of phonics for teaching children to read*. New York: Morrow.

STEVENS, G.D. and BIRCH, J.W. (1957) A proposal for clarification of the terminology used to describe brain injured children. *Exceptional Children*, **23**, 346–349.

STRAUSS, A.A. (1933 a) Beitraege zur einteilung, entstehung und klinik der schwersten schwachsinnsformen. *Archiv fur Psychiatrie*, **99**, 693.

STRAUSS, A.A. (1933 b) Heilpaedagogik und klinik. *Zeitschrift fur Kinderforschung*, **41**, 445–454.

STRAUSS, A.A. (1938, November 12) *Effects of exogenous factors in the organism as a whole in mentally deficient children*. Paper presented at the biennial meeting of the Society for Research in Child Development.

STRAUSS, A.A. and KEPHART, N.C. (1955) *Psychopathology and education of the brain-injured child: Vol. II, progress in theory and clinic*. New York: Grune and Stratton.

STRAUSS, A.A. and LEHTINEN, L.E. (1947) *Psychopathology and education of the brain-injured child*. New York: Grune and Stratton.

STRAUSS, A.A. and WERNER, H. (1941) The mental organization of the brain-injured mentally defective child. *American Journal of Psychiatry*, **97**, 1194–1202.

TARVER, S. and HALLAHAN, D.P. (1976) Children with learning disabilities: An overview. In J.M. KAUFFMAN and D.P. HALLAHAN (Eds), *Teaching children with learning disabilities: Personal perspectives* (pp. 2–57). Columbus, OH: Merrill.

THOMAS, C.J. (1905) Congenital word-blindness and its treatment. *Ophthalmoscope*, **3**, 380.

TOMLINSON, S. (1982) *A sociology of special education*. London: Routledge and Kegan Paul.

TURNBULL, A.P. and SCHULZ, J.B. (1979) *Mainstreaming handicapped students: A guide for the classroom teacher*. Boston: Allyn and Bacon.

UNITED STATES OFFICE OF SPECIAL EDUCATION AND REHABILITATIVE SERVICES. (1984) *Sixth annual report to Congress on the implementation of Public Law 94–142: The education for all handicapped children act.* Washington, DC: U.S. Department of Education. (The fifth annual report was published 1983).

WARNER, W.L., HAVIGHURST, R.J. and LOEB, M.L. (1944) *Who shall be educated?: The challenge of unequal opportunities.* New York and London: Harper.

WASSERMAN, M. (1974) Collective versus individual purpose: Beyond freeschooling and deschooling [Introduction]. In G. CHANAN and L. GILCHRIST, *What school is for* (pp. vii–xxii). New York: Praeger.

WEATHERLEY, R.A. (1979) *Reforming special education: Policy implementation from state level to street level.* Cambridge, MA: MIT Press.

WECHSLER, D. (1949) *Manual: Wechsler intelligence scale for children.* New York: The Psychological Corporation.

WECHSLER, D. (1974) *Manual: Wechsler intelligence scale for children — Revised.* New York: The Psychological Corporation.

WEPMAN, J.M. (1958) *Auditory discrimination test.* Chicago: Language Research Associates.

WEPMAN, J.M. (1960) Auditory discrimination, speech and reading. *Elementary School Journal,* **60**, 245–247.

WERNER, H. and STRAUSS, A.A. (1940) Pathology of the figure-ground relation in the child. *Psychological Bulletin,* **37**, 440. (Presentation at the 48th annual meeting of the American Psychological Association at Pennsylvania State College, September 4–7).

WERNICKE, C. (1874) *Der aphasische symptomencomplex.* Breslau: Tasche.

WEST, T.L. and BATES, P. (1977) Mainstreaming: An overview. In P. BATES, T.L. WEST and R.B. SCHMERL (Eds), *Mainstreaming: Problems, potentials, and perspectives* (pp. 7–22). Minneapolis, MN: National Support Systems Project.

WIEDERHOLT, J.L. (1974) Historical perspectives on the education of the learning disabled. In L. MANN and D.A. SABATINO (Eds.), *The second review of special education* (pp. 103–152). Philadelphia: JSE Press.

WINSLOW, R. (1982, February 21) College for the learning disabled. *The New York Times Magazine,* pp. 80, 87, 90–91.

WITKIN, H.A. (1965) Heinz Werner: 1890–1964. *Child Development,* **36**, 306–328.

WOLMAN, B.B. (Ed.). (1973) *Dictionary of behavioral science.* New York: Van Nostrand Reinhold.

WOZNIAK, R.H. (1975) Psychology and education of the learning disabled child in the Soviet Union. In W.M. CRUICKSHANK and D.P. HALLAHAN (Eds), *Perceptual and learning disabilities in children: Vol. 1, psychoeducational practices* (pp. 407–479). Syracuse, NY: Syracuse University Press.

YOUNG, M.F.D. (Ed.). (1971) *Knowledge and control: New directions for the sociology of education.* London: Routledge and Kegan Paul.

YOUNIE, W.J. (1967) *Instructional approaches to slow learning.* New York: Teachers College Press.

YSSELDYKE, J.E. and ALGOZZINE, B. (1982) *Critical issues in special and remedial education.* Boston: Houghton Mifflin.

YSSELDYKE, J.E., ALGOZZINE, B., SHINN, M.R. and McGUE, M. (1982) Similarities and differences between low achievers and students classified learning disabled. *Journal of Special Education,* **16**, 73–85.

ZILBOORG, G. and HENRY, G.W. (1941) *History of medical psychology.* New York: Norton.

Index